Small Victories

The Off-Camera Life of an On-Camera Mom

by Molly Grantham

This book is an original production of Miss Meade Publishing
Charlotte, NC
Copyright ©2017 by Molly Grantham

Cover design by Diana Wade
Text design by Diana Wade
Cover photography by Emby Taylor

I have tried to recreate events, locales, and conversations from my memories of them. I have only used the first initial of a person's last name when quoting their post from a pubic Facebook page.

ISBN: 978-0-9994302-0-0

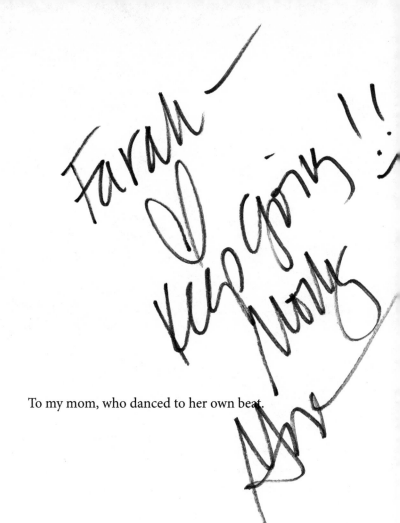

To my mom, who danced to her own beat.

THE INTRO TO THE INTRO

I like working sometimes more than I like being a mom.

I wonder how many of you now think something horrible about me.

I wonder how many of you understand.

Enjoying my fifty-plus hours a week away from home does not take away from how much I love my kids. My six-year-old daughter Parker is happy, healthy, funny, stubborn, melodramatic, thoughtful, wickedly smart, and tests every boundary. She sweetly practices curtsies in her favorite princess dress, terrorizes the dog by riding her scooter through the house with untouchable fearlessness, and at times acts more adult than I do.

Two-year-old Hutch has eyes bluer than any ocean. They light up in every photo. He smiles big and laughs from his gut, which is huge. He is never full, always wants more of everything, stands up for himself against his strong-willed older sister, and can turn on tears like an actor. The moment those blues water, an unsuspecting rookie gives him whatever he wants. He's learning the art of manipulation, is more cuddly than any child I've ever come across, and never wants to let me go.

My daughter matters, my son matters, and my job matters.

One of those three things is not like the other two, but all are pieces of me.

There are women who thrive in corporate settings—I'm one of them. Usually we multitask at a crazy level, battle problems with control, and have minds like calendars that DoNotStop. We're also good friends, listeners, overachievers, perfectionists, and generally take on other people's problems as our own. We solve things. We own things. We like to be liked, but can be incredibly authoritative. "Effortless" is a constant goal and major compliment.

I guess that's why it took me so long to surrender to motherhood— I didn't want to feel like I was giving any of that up.

I'm an evening news anchor and investigative reporter at WBTV News, the almost seventy-year-old CBS affiliate in Charlotte, North Carolina. I *like* writing and reporting about drugs, crime, controversial social issues, and illness. I *never* expected to enjoy writing about my kids.

But life changes. It evolves.

I know that now.

The greatest thing I ever accidentally did was write down what was in my head on Week One of maternity leave with Hutch, then follow up in a grassroots way in the weeks and months afterward. I happened to put my thoughts on Facebook, but the point isn't where you record them, it's when you later go back and read them straight through. The change by Month Thirty, when Hutch was two and a half and Parker was turning six, jumped off the pages. I matured as they did, and everyone who commented on the Facebook posts helped me see the growth by adding perspective.

Maybe those words can help another parent, too. I went through the thousands of Facebook comments and am including some of my favorites in this book.

I hope that in reading these entries and essays of a reluctant mom who adores her kids, you laugh, share a relatable moment or two, and maybe most of all take comfort in the beautiful truth life provides.

—Molly

INTRODUCTION

I grew up assuming I'd someday be a parent. By the age of thirty-three I still had no thoughts about making those kids happen.

My husband, Wes, and I didn't want to add new variables into the equation. Not yet. We were too busy living full days. Even though we'd always envisioned nameless little silhouettes in our future, I had zero desire to be pregnant.

Which might be why I didn't know I was, until eleven and a half weeks along.

I know: *how did I not know* I had another heart beating inside me? I've given this serious thought. In retrospect, I had been stressed in those months, had no morning sickness, am always up and down five pounds, and because I had no intention of being pregnant, it didn't cross my mind I might be.

I'm not proud of my stone-cold reaction when I went to a routine checkup and heard my doctor excitedly say, "You're going to have a baby!" And I hate remembering how hesitant I was to tell my boss. I'd just gotten a promotion and thought he'd be bitter. He wasn't. A little surprised, but not angry.

There was one moment though, when a male coworker, who I don't think knew how he sounded, told me being pregnant would be "good for your career—it'll soften you."

That chauvinistic comment solidified my personal vow to not let pregnancy change my work ethic. I didn't want to act any differently, and didn't want people to treat me differently. I wanted to be Molly. Always. Mother or not.

With that as my mantra, I kept up being a bulldog journalist as the months ticked on. I went into a high-security prison to sit across from a violent rapist and ask probing questions in order to educate on the mindset of criminals like him. This was also the time of Charlotte's "Trial of the Decade"—the man who killed two Charlotte-Mecklenburg police officers in cold blood. I covered it from start to finish. Separately, six dangerous MS-13 gang members went to federal court. I'd formed solid sources over the years, even traveling to South Central Los Angeles, and was able to use their deep knowledge to show the consequences of this case, the law, and the danger gangs pose to everyone in Charlotte.

That year I was named Reporter of the Year for the Carolinas by RTDNAC, all while growing as big as a house. Way more important than any award, I was proud of my work. The pregnancy hadn't slowed me down.

Because of all those heavy headlines and daily phone calls and constant source texts, it was easy to never take the time to stop and THINK about what was happening inside of me. I never got a *What to Expect* book. Wes and I never went to tour the hospital or take a Lamaze class. I considered registering for baby stuff as another check on a daily to-do list, but didn't have one thought about what bringing home all this new stuff—plus an actual baby—would mean for our lives.

It is no more obvious how obtuse I was being than the day our daughter was born. In the weeks before her due date, I was working on a story about an elderly firecracker of a woman who had killed her husband decades before in self-defense. He was wildly abusive (old pictures and witnesses proved it), and in a small South Carolina town where he was buddies with law enforcement, she didn't stand a chance. She served twenty years in prison for murdering a man she felt certain would kill her and her children. Now she was in her seventies, wanting off probation.

A producer and I went with this woman to her probation hearing. Her ex-husband's family showed as well. I'm summarizing here, but they essentially said, "She deserved the abuse," then tore into us for reporting the case. Our camera was rolling as they verbally attacked. Ultimately, she was up against too much hate in an antiquated system and the probation board denied her request.

The story's airdate was set for April 6 on the 11 p.m. show. The baby's due date wasn't until April 12. Perfect, I thought. Days to spare.

Except, I woke up feeling weird the morning of April 6. Wes and I went to the doctor, who said I was in labor. I told my doctor I HAD to be at work fourteen hours later. He said nothing for a minute, then explained labor could last three hours or two days, and suggested I proceed as normal until the shooting pains were ten minutes apart. (He later told me he'd thought I was kidding about working, and that pause was him realizing I wasn't.)

I went in early afternoon to start my night shift. Around 4 p.m. the baby kicked it up a notch. I ignored it and went to anchor the show while having sporadic contractions. Typing that now sounds a little ridiculous, but it's the truth. About ten minutes in, co-anchor Jamie Boll, a father of four, turned to me in a commercial break. I was breathing heavily.

"Molly," he said firmly. "I am not interested in being your coach. GO TO THE HOSPITAL."

We chuckle about that to this day.

At 6 p.m. when the show was over, three of my girlfriends were waiting outside the studio. News had spread. We all knew I wouldn't make it to 11 p.m. I insisted on sending a final email about how to end the story I now wouldn't be there to tell, and went to my car.

While driving home to let Wes get us to the hospital, I called the oldest of my younger brothers. He humored me. (Endless credit to all three of my brothers: each one always humors me.) Jay listened for a while, eventually telling me he was counting my contractions over the phone.

Granted he was a new dad, but I hadn't thought to time anything.

At the hospital, an epidural slowed things down. At 11 p.m. the doctor finally said it was time. First, I said, I wanted us to watch a little news.

"Good evening. I'm Paul Cameron," my partner began. He gave a pointed smile. "Molly's NOT HERE."

And just like that, everyone watching knew exactly where I was.

The story I'd been working on so hard was introduced shortly, and all of us in the delivery room, doctor included, watched this woman's fight for a pardon and her tears of injustice. At the end, Paul perfectly relayed that final email I'd sent. We'd gotten it done.

Having the story over calmed me. It let me let go and focus on the bigger picture at hand.

Right after midnight, Parker Meade was born.

Later, as the sun was rising, I was holding this hours-old beautiful little bundle. She was scrunched and slightly yellow and nestled into my arms. Wes was asleep on the couch. I was alone with Parker, waiting for that feeling. That one movies and commercials say washes over you as a new mom. I was staring at her, anticipating unconditional love to burst open my soul with a sensation I'd never experienced.

Only, it wasn't coming. I was fascinated with her features and liked looking at her little nose, but I wasn't bathed in glorious emotions. I started to question myself: What is wrong with me? There had to be something wrong. Everyone says having a baby changes your life, but I didn't feel any major difference. I started to panic...maybe I shouldn't tell anyone she was here yet? How could I share this teeny-tiny thing as my new, perfect daughter if I wasn't even feeling motherly?

At that critical mental moment I got a text from friend Keith

Larson. At the time he had a morning radio show at our sister station and had me on regularly to talk about my stories.

"Did you have the baby?"

"Yes. A girl." I kept my reply short.

"Moll! What's her name? Everyone okay?"

Basic questions to read, but they felt heavy.

"Parker Meade. All seems good."

"Can I announce it?" I got why he was asking. Of course his listeners would want to know. I'd been on his show just two days before. He'd even played "Guess Molly's Surprise" with callers when I finally realized I was pregnant.

Could he announce it? Well, yes, I guess. Even though I felt unsure about the whole thing, it was no doubt happy news. We were healthy! She was a miracle, and I didn't want anyone thinking something was wrong. I texted back that he could, which then spurred me to call WBTV as well. They sent cameras into the hospital. Eleven hours after Parker was born, we were on television. It was followed up the next day with a blurb in the *Charlotte Observer.*

All of that required me to act excited and smiley, and none of that felt natural.

ೞೈಞ

I confess the details of that story about Parker's arrival, to help explain how unprepared I was for kids. I've always loved children, had a babysitting business in junior high and was a nanny one summer, but it took me time to wave the white flag to motherhood. Parker's baby announcement was a prime example. I used a sweet black-and-white picture of our Wonderdog mutt kissing her forehead with custom-printed pink font that read, *Fisher's New Toy*. Without realizing it, I made our daughter's birth more about the dog than her.

It didn't stop there. When Parker was three weeks old, Wes went on a work trip. I told him to go, but once he was gone I was irritated. Bored. Fidgety. I wanted to be traveling, too. So I got online and booked a beach condo, and when she was five weeks old, we packed virtually every piece of new baby equipment for her first trip to the ocean. At ten weeks, I was full-on  back into reading every morning headline, and when she was eleven weeks old, I drove her six hours to meet up with a bunch of my college girlfriends for a weekend reunion. There are pictures of ten of us girls gabbing around a kitchen counter with Parker lying in the middle of the island, content, staring up at the lights.

Examples of that kind of restlessness followed me through maternity leave. I distracted myself from being a mother because I didn't know what to do with time home alone, an unscheduled baby to hold, and zero emails to process. I felt comfortable with her and could feel myself falling in love by the day, but also felt like

I needed more.

When those three months of time off were over, I was grateful to get back into the bustle of a newsroom. I dove in focused. Like a dog on a bone, I started reporting on CBD oils (cannabis oils, a strain of medical marijuana) ultimately helping determined parents of kids who needed these oils change North Carolina law.

People asked about Parker. I was proud, but not chatty. I'd somehow get into a different conversation. I could talk endlessly about what was happening in the world, but still couldn't—and didn't—talk much about my real life beyond the camera.

Plus, no one wanted to hear the truth about how much I enjoyed spending the mornings with her (she was growing so fast!), but how easy it was for me to head to work every afternoon.

Then I got pregnant again. Wes and I only told a handful of people. I was happy to give Parker a sibling—I love my own brothers with such deep devotion I knew I wanted to give her the opportunity to cultivate a similar relationship—but still wasn't ready for the attention that announcing a pregnancy brings.

Around the end of the first trimester, Wes and I went to the doctor's office for a normal appointment. While lying down with that cold jelly on my stomach, the tech got silent. She kept moving the ultrasound wand over my abdomen. She asked me to hold on a minute and left the room. Another tech returned with her, who also took many minutes to move the wand around. They finally looked at us sadly and said they couldn't hear a heartbeat.

"What does that mean?" I asked. I didn't get it.

"It means you miscarried," one of them said. "For whatever reason, the baby died."

Oh.

The baby died.

Oh.

Was it something I did wrong?

"No!" they assured. "This happens to one in four women."

I never talk about my miscarriage. Some of my closest friends are probably reading this, surprised. But why shouldn't we be talking about it? To have *one in four women* go through the process of creating life, to carry it inside them, only to know that life died, and then to have it removed, with a machine, and then to have to get yourself emotionally and physically okay with either starting or not starting that whole process over again? That anguish and mental struggle is worth an honest discussion. And though I didn't and don't talk about the miscarriage often, when I do actually go down that path I end up hearing story after story after story from other women about their own miscarriages. One friend of mine even told me she had four.

I had no idea.

After that I once again threw myself into work.

CR80

About a year later I found out I was pregnant again. This time, a boy. He was due one day before Komen Charlotte's *Race for the Cure*, an annual breast cancer 5K I love to emcee. My doctor and nurse signed up for the race in case I went into labor that morning, because baby or no baby, I told them I was going to be there. (Same doctor. He understood.)

Pictures from that morning accurately show an overdue pregnant workaholic hugging survivors and happily running around with her three-and-a-half-year-old.

Hutch Thomas was born the following Saturday. Eight days late and in no hurry to go anywhere, a personality trait he still owns.

It was during my maternity leave with Hutch that something inside me changed, and it happened almost instantly. One child hadn't slapped me silly with the realization of a new normal, but two did. The difference in our lives was immediate. There were no waiting bouquets when we arrived home. Wes didn't take any time off this go-round. It was just me, with no fanfare, no special serenade, still medically fragile, trying to care for an incredibly hungry infant and a precocious, active, attention-grabbing little girl. Forget "needing more," like I had on Parker's maternity leave. I was feeling trapped by all I had.

That first week…oh, that first week. I felt pulled in a hundred uneasy directions. I didn't know my own self. Everything was off-kilter. I felt victorious just finding time to shower. So victorious, in fact, I jotted it down:

"Showered today. Small victory."

I timidly copied that proud thought to Facebook. I had a push to share the feeling, even though I thought shouting out such a menial accomplishment might be ridiculous. I looked at the post a full minute before cries came from another room needing attention.

With no time to think, I pressed Publish, and put down the phone.

When I looked at my Facebook page later, I was floored. People had responded. Putting the words down had made me feel like me. But reaction from others—a reaction of support and knowing what I was going through—made me want to share something again the following week.

The posts became my written comfort food. Every week I'd go through these struggles of spending every second of every day around a three-and-a-half-year-old and a hungry newborn while my husband went off to work, and every week I'd spit something out on Facebook that felt true inside.

At first it was list-based thoughts because early on, that's the only bandwidth a new parent has available. I'd type the bullet points on my phone one-handed while simultaneously nursing or pumping. There were days I couldn't even leave the house, and I started to look forward to any moment I'd get a chance to document the daily frustrations and joys cluttering my head to a moving world outside. They became my medicine to making me feel like me.

As time went on and I adjusted to parenting two, my narratives got longer.

The affirmations and personal stories in response—whether pithy, supportive, endearing, or questioning my own parenting tactics—helped me realize I wasn't alone and kept me connected to a community. The comments made me realize I was lowering the guard we all have up: trying to be perfect, and never complain, and never question.

The weeks of leave blurred, and then, after three months, it was time to go back to work. But this time I got back into a newsroom and felt the exact opposite of what I'd felt after my first leave. Now I missed sharing the life I had as a mom.

I decided to start writing again. With a fifty-hour-a-week job, I knew I'd have to switch to monthly updates (and maybe a post or two in between?), thinking someday Parker and Hutch would be old enough to read them and enjoy knowing what our lives were like when they were little. These monthly excerpts, I thought, could serve as a digital scrapbook. Not totally shiny, but real.

It started as Small Victories. It has grown into a way to collect stories for new parents, old parents, and anyone who wants a glimpse into the life of a mom trying to do her best.

Enjoy the journey ahead...

...I've enjoyed living it.

OCTOBER

WEEK ONE: Small Victories

My normal is gone. At least temporarily. I'm not spending my days writing stories, anchoring shows, or working events, where productivity is seen with instant results. Instead, I'm starting a marathon. Marathons aren't really my thing. I like big progress, not drips into a glass you're trying to fill. But in these seven days since the birth of my son the only thing I can see are tiny successes.

Like showering.

I showered today.

Small victory.

I've decided that small victories in these first weeks should count just as much as corporate-world accomplishments. So here goes. I'm listing mine in an effort to comfort any other parent currently in the same spot.

SMALL VICTORIES:

- Finding time to shower. (I got one every day, thank you.)
- Was given the all-clear to drive again. Freedom!
- Installed two car seats.
- Wrote six thank-you cards.
- Got Hutch to doctor. Am getting him to gain weight.
- Found time to call some agency about a birth certificate.
- Got most out-of-state family in for a visit.
- Got them back out.
- Allotted quality arts-and-crafts happy time with Parker.
- Glitter everywhere. I didn't yell.
- (Deserving of own bullet point.)
- Brushed up on math: How many ounces in how many hours?
- Confirmed a haircut appointment.
- Kept my sanity with two to three hours of sleep a night.
- Mostly.
- Kept my sanity, mostly.

THINGS I LEFT UNTOUCHED:

- Friends.
- Laundry.
- Email.
- Wine (two glasses in seven days does not count).

NEXT WEEK'S GOALS:
- Get actual birth certificate.
- Get to that haircut appointment.
- Buy more coffee for at-home maker.
- Continue to make it all work.

Sending more power to new parents, once again new, or first time. Funny, real, honest or a bit frustrating…our small victories add up to something big.

COMMENTS:

Ashley H. My small victory…Pink shirt, pink pants, pink socks and pink hair for pink day at daughter's school…it all came together.

James B. Molly, my wife's small victory was taking care of a three year old, a newborn daughter, and a husband who had surgery. Super moms do what they must.

Becky C. My baby #4 is 11 weeks. I ran a 5K this morning! I may be insane. I also got to shower. My parents fed my older kids too much sugar. They then became crazy and fought the rest of the day. Hubby working late. We all survived til bed time!

Lindsay O. This was my small victory this week: getting both of my children to sit still so I could paint their feet to make this. (My one year old squirmed a little, which is why he has 6 toes on both feet in the picture!) Ha!

WEEK TWO: Time

The reality of clock management during newbornhood…I'd forgotten. Time works against you. The fact I'm not posting about Week Two until we're already into Week Three seems fitting.

An hour can feel like the length of a weekend, without the downtime.

Going somewhere takes twenty minutes instead of five because of how many checklists are in your mind of what to pack, carry, grab, and how it impacts naptime. It's exhausting just to get out the door. Feedings are endless.

Then…suddenly…the three-year-old is with a friend and the baby fell asleep on the couch. (You realize he's now the exact length of two remote controls.) YOU HAVE AN HOUR TO YOURSELF. Oh my gosh! AN HOUR!? Should I email? Do laundry? Hit the grocery store? Sleep? (No way—sleep is overrated.) I'd love to write. I had a book title I wanted to send a friend. Should I call her? Some thank-you notes I need to get out, and a couple of headlines this morning caught my eye.

Is now the time to take a real look? YES! A FULL HOUR!

I think about what to do while organizing clutter. Takes ten minutes.

Then…though I've only started two emails and one load of clothes but not checked any actual item off the list…then…no. Please, no. But, yes. That IS someone crying. Or, that IS Parker needing me. Or, that IS my mom calling and I must answer. But, we only just started the clock. How can the hour of pseudo-independence be done? It lasted a heartbreakingly short twenty-four minutes and all I have to show is a picked-up downstairs.

Time. It's not dependable. Not able to be halved or quartered, adaptable or understanding of your new world.

GRATEFUL IN WEEK TWO FOR:
- Friends.
- They remind me of the waiting world.
- Multitasking.
- Clean sheets.
- Showers. Still one a day.
- Postponing jury duty (again).
- Thoughts at 3 a.m. (I'm writing this on my phone at 3:19 a.m.)
- The fact I'm exceptionally good at one-handed text-typing.
- The 3% of my closet starting to fit.
- Parker's acceptance over sharing her life with a new someone.
- Her one-liners:
- "Mommy, does Thai food have things in knots?"
- Routines. (Ballet class! Early voting! Metrolina this week!)

- The way Hutch crunches his nose and purses his lips when full.
- His weight gain.
- Onesies with zippers.
- Pretty days.
- Nearby parks.
- A rocking porch swing.
- The Shutterfly app for pictures.
- Homemade, super-soft blankets.
- The human body. He's magic. How did I carry and create life?

FRUSTRATIONS:

- The human body. Magic is out of me. What's this extra weight?
- Solicitors who ring the doorbell in the face of a screaming note: *PLEASE KNOCK.*
- Paperwork.
- Women you don't know who ask your "birthing story."
- Women you don't know who follow that up with theirs.
- Onesies with buttons.
- Power outages.
- The other 97% of my closet I can't get into.

GOALS:

- Return at least two phone calls.
- Create 28 hours in a day.
- Schedule *nothing* when scoring those extra four.

I do know I looked at the time when I began typing with my left hand (with Hutch in the other arm as we rock) and no matter why I'm really writing, I believe I used these thirty-two minutes wisely.

COMMENTS:

Glenda B. Sadly no one tells you two children does not DOUBLE your responsibilities but more like QUADRUPLES them.

Trish E. Watch out for Week Three. The hormones skyrocket and plummet—if you find yourself a scattered mess, can't get it together or suddenly crying—take a long nap with the kids. You are overdoing. There is not a prize for being super mom.

Lynn B. A long time ago, a girlfriend had just had her third baby in 30 months. Her observation: The difference between one child and two is the difference between one and twelve. A third just means Surrender, Dorothy…they win. Go with it. You're doing great—and really articulate for 3 a.m. typing on a phone! Kudos.

Jennifer H. Thanks for sharing your weeks with us. My two week old doesn't like to sleep at 3 a.m. Totally feel the "hour"! Can't wait for Week Three…

NOVEMBER

WEEK THREE: Accomplishment

You don't normally get three weeks into something and think, "Time to pat myself on the back." Accomplishment usually comes at a set marker—maybe a year-end review, or when an award is given.

Awards should be handed out to sleepless parents.

Just twenty-three days ago was Night One. Can any adult inching through weeks of newbornhood imagine starting over? In three weeks Hutch has gained two pounds. He jumped from sleeping two hours in between night feedings to a blessed four. Parker has now become used to sharing the back row with another car seat. The dog realizes the baby  isn't leaving. I have all gear organized. I even got out shopping this week with him sleeping on my chest as I walked around.

I can't imagine being back at square one.

For anyone thinking, "Come on now, three weeks isn't a long stretch," you're right. In the normal world it's not. But during newbornhood, three weeks feels like four months. The shininess of having a "new baby" is gone. You're getting into a daily groove. You know there's a long way to go and any one day can be explosively bad, but surviving three weeks feels like turning an invisible corner.

I keep wanting someone to tell me, "YOU'RE DOING IT. Your twenty-four-hour cycle might be missing a clear beginning and end...but YOU'RE GETTING THERE. You're not just a milk factory; you are a human being ACCOMPLISHING big things!"

Because no one is telling me that, I'm telling you. It feels great to type.

In that vein, I'm dedicating this week to "Sanity Savers"—things that help you get there. Like those savvy little disposable microwavable bags that sanitize everything in two minutes, and really, really good coffee. The easy reading of Facebook falls into this category, as do adult conversations, Motrin, the grocery aisles inside Target (one-stop shopping), friends who take your older kid out for an afternoon, wool socks, and boxed Kraft macaroni and cheese.

The restaurant KO Sushi. You order online, talk to no one, and they deliver to your door. Chick-fil-A's applesauce option is also a Sanity Saver, as well as the $15 Walmart CD player in Parker's room, providing her hours of solo dance entertainment.

Rounding out the list of helpers on exceptionally blurry days: bath toys, space heaters, new diapers that change colors if peed in (no more "finger checks"), and a glass of wine. Or two. Or three. Pump and dump, baby.

Lots of "strikeouts" this week, too. I want to be honest in listing both sides. I never got a Halloween costume for Hutch. Never got a picture of Parker in hers. I took the kids outside to play in 40-degree weather and, after ten minutes of crying, finally figured out I didn't have shoes on either of them. Poor Hutch had blue toes. I also didn't start a diet and full-on forgot preschool picture day. Parker looked homeless.

And on we roll.

COMMENTS:

Donna W. Three weeks with a new infant should bring rewards and standing ovations. You manage to know their names, your own address and what is needed to get accomplished.

Nicole R.

My Sanity Savers:

A very helpful 7-year-old.

A semi helpful 6-year-old.

Bath time for myself while husband hangs with the baby.

My Strikeouts:

A wannabe helpful 1-year-old.

My homework, because I thought it was smart to take a couple classes and have a newborn in the same semester.

Marian W. My favorite was missing picture day & Parker looking homeless. I laughed out loud. Hutch is a doll! Have a little more wine!

WEEK FOUR: "Pollyanna Says…"

Your entire day (and night) is spent with a three-and-a-half-year-old and newborn? Not exactly a recipe for relaxation. Especially when your subconscious knows no miracle Mary Poppins is on her way to assist.

You know there will be a time when you will miss this. You know you'll look back and remember the one or two sweet moments in each agonizingly long day, as opposed to the dozens of not-quite-as-sweet moments.

I understand that many people call these weeks "bliss." I do not. I love these two babies in an unconditional way, but the days aren't full of sunshine and daffodils with angels singing. I'm still living every hour with a three-year-old tornado and a four-week-old (one month today) who I swear eats more than me.

Which is why I started channeling Pollyanna.

Example: Find a full teacup of curdled milk secretly stashed behind Parker's plastic playroom table? Instead of throwing up at the smell—the milk is two weeks old—channel Pollyanna. "What a great discovery," good ol' Polly says. "Now I know why the room had that peculiar odor, and I can fix the problem!"

Example: Hutch violently vomits all four ounces of milk he finally gets down. Do you groan? No! You channel Polly. "Nice aim, Hutch. It's ONLY all over me and my new shirt. You missed the furniture. Less to clean!"

Example: I'm giving Parker a bath while feeding Hutch. Simultaneously. She's in the tub, he's in my arms as I kneel beside it. She stands up trying to kindly throw bubbles from her cupped hands at his mouth to make him look like "Baby Santa" with a beard. I don't have enough arms to make her sit down, so now there's a pool of water on the floor, a screaming month-old because soap tastes bad, and a cursing mother. Pollyanna pops in the mind: "Well, you could've had twins."

With two babies, cold weather, and long days of maternity leave, ludicrous is everywhere. That's why Pollyanna is my new best girlfriend. Instead of screaming or crying every time, I invite her perspective. She manages to make me hate her cheeriness instead of the actual situation at hand.

COMMENTS:

Joanie S. So glad that you are letting women know it's ok to say it isn't all sunshine and roses. Too many mothers feel inept because society tells them that they are not allowed to feel overwhelmed and frustrated. It's okay to keep it real.

Mandy S. I have triplet 4 year olds and a 9-month-old. Totally relate and I often try to channel Mary Poppins in hopes of spit-spot magic cleaning. Guess I'll try Pollyanna for good thoughts.

Katie L. Let me give you something to look forward to: our four children just gave us time at a beautiful bed and breakfast, a wonderful dinner, and beautiful flowers in our suite. We were celebrating our 60th anniversary, and, needless to say, it added one more wonderful memory to a lifetime of special memories. Hang in there!

Sabrina C. Where were you 6 years ago while I was going through the same thing?

WEEK FIVE: Wash. Rinse. Repeat.

I find myself once again sitting in the quiet of a feeding, one-handedly texting myself an email to turn into a post. What do I say about this past Week Five? It's not like anything is massively different. It's still heart-filling, awesome, and challenging. I still channel Pollyanna. I'm still counting small victories. I still wonder why time works against parents of newborns.

Guess upon reflection, Week Five is just more of the same.

Or is it?

This past week, Hutch smiled at me. I don't know if he tried to do it, but I'm counting it as legitimate. He also did his first projectile poop. Not fun, but all new in his young life. In a more pleasant recollection, while he napped today I got a never-before chance to teach Parker how to cook in the kitchen—nothing better on a rainy day than making a gooey grilled cheese.

Finding the funny is also a part of Week Five. Things like having both kids at the hair salon for my much-needed appointment. I sat in Miss Tiffany's chair with my dark roots, holding a sassy Parker, who in turn insisted she hold twelve-pound Hutch. All while getting foils put in the top of my head. If you can't laugh at yourself, you've got nothing.

Week Five also felt like going through the motions. Same three hours in a row, eight different times a day: Nap. Feed. Play. Nap. Feed. Play. Nap. Feed. Play.

Now that I sit with a moment to breathe, and think (and breathe, and breathe, and breathe, ahhhh...), I'm wondering if the sensation of repeating a daily cycle might actually mean something good.

Maybe the fact that you have to look harder for milestones is an indication you're adjusting better to your new normal.

COMMENTS:

Sara L.C. The picture at the hair salon is priceless!

Judy F. I love the sizes of the hands. Your mom hands, the infant hands and most precious of all, young Parker cradling her brother's head so tenderly in her young hands. Nothing to laugh at with this photo. It's all beauty.

Alcy P. I involved my kids in life from day one, too! They learn life that way, and how to be respectful. Teaches them about life, not hiding them from it.

Vicki VDF. Takes a woman who is confident in herself to post a picture with foil on her head.

WEEK SIX: Walking the Line

Week Six leaves me feeling like I have one foot stuck in the real world, and one foot elsewhere. I can do a string of errands, but it takes twice as long. I'm returning phone calls, but often have to cut conversations short. I got to go on my first Saturday night out with friends, but returned home only to stay up most of the night with a child who wouldn't sleep.

Hutch is not to blame. Three-year-old Parker is making her six-week-old brother seem like a hibernating bear. Her new obsession is creating excuses about how she can't stay in her own bed. Last night I swear she dumped half a bottle of water on herself at 3:45 a.m., and then hysterically told me she had no idea how everything got wet, but she [big gulp of air] needed [big crocodile tears and gulp of air] to get [big gulp of air and flailing arms] new pajamas, and [cue total breakdown] in bed with me.

I won't be sleepless forever. Every parent knows stages come and go. I just wasn't expecting *her* nighttime obstacles.

Which proves my Week Six theory: BECAUSE you're more into a routine...BECAUSE you're starting to dip back into the real life of you...BECAUSE you're getting into a groove and feeling like "I got this"...now is when karma kicks in and tosses a few more balls to juggle.

NOW is when the balance of newbornhood and real life blur and you stand caught between the two.

Any parent who is at all functioning at this point should realize they're kicking butt and taking names, even if they don't feel full throttle. Six weeks isn't two years. The bar can remain slightly lower. Perfection isn't the goal; there's credit in just getting a task complete. Getting something checked off the list—no matter how you do it—is perfectly acceptable.

Like yesterday. I got to Parker's ballet class. It shouldn't matter that I forgot her shoes. I made it there and watched her dance (barefoot) for 45 minutes through that dang little window.

For any parent living this life, remember: you're you...but cut yourself a break if you're not totally the same you quite yet.

COMMENTS:

Erin B. You make me terrified and excited to become a mom all at the same time.

Loyd P. How much better the world would be if all parents took their responsibilities as seriously and yet knew it was important to laugh at themselves. It is a gift you will certainly pass on to your children that will be treasured above everything else. And for the record, my youngest is 20 years old and seven hours away, and there are still nights I don't sleep.

Dorian S. Typical reaction from your daughter. She is probably a bit jealous of her brother.

Chris M. I haven't slept through the night in 18 years. (Mine are 18 and 16.)

Erica P. My baby girl will be six weeks old tomorrow. I relate!

Tiffany S. Best mommy advice I have: do not let her sleep with you. Tough it out. Ask me about my 10-year-old next time I see you at the salon. –Miss Tiffany

DECEMBER

WEEK SEVEN: Unproductive Productivity

This morning I got Parker dressed and packed her lunchbox for school. We were almost ready to go when she, Hutch, and I had an unexpected cuddle on the couch. I passed out with them in my arms. Wes took a photo before walking out the door. He texted it on the way to work and the buzz of the phone woke me up. Needless to say, Parker was twenty minutes late.

Oh, well.

Before going on maternity leave with Parker three years ago, I falsely believed the three months I'd have off would be more time to spend on projects, clean closets, update address books, and maybe even finish writing one of the many short stories I'd started. Like a little vacation at home. I was wrong.

This go-round, I knew there wouldn't be more time, but I guess I forgot how a day that is jam-packed can also *feel* unproductive.

For instance, I'm writing this from the bottom bunk in Parker's bedroom. I'm here because this afternoon my never-naps three-year-old actually suggested she and I "take a rest together." I wasn't about to pass up the opportunity. She wanted the top bunk; I'm left wasting thirty minutes here on the bottom hoping she'll fall asleep. (I just heard her talk to a stuffed animal, so no success yet.) Point being…with a newborn and three-year-old, you can be busy every hour, yet have totally empty minutes.

"What did you do today, Molly?"

"Oh, I looked at wooden planks underneath a mattress while listening to a made-up conversation Parker moderated between Brown Bear, Silly Dog, and Pinky the Rabbit."

Not exactly something to check off a to-do list. (Sidebar: Why does a to-do list grow AS you're unable to do anything about it? I am quietly stuck on this bunk mentally adding items: call and fight with the manufacturer of our broken baby monitor…order Christmas cards…plan a January trip with brothers…make the Goodwill pile…get Hutch on a rigid schedule…figure out childcare for jury duty next week…blah, blah, blah.)

Here's the truth: I miss me. I miss the me that ran around putting more into twenty-four hours than most. I miss emails and interviewing people and making editorial decisions. I miss the responsibility of work tasks that aren't as long-term important as what I'm doing every day right now with my kids, but feel more short-term rewarding when completed.

It's easy to miss those parts of me that I love.

Those thoughts come as I sit staring at the bottom of a bunk, but they're not taking permanent residence in my mind. Parker's voice pushes them away. I'm listening to her imagination dream up a field trip where she's taking her stuffed friends to the zoo. Some pretty high entertainment. (She just told Pinky, "After we go to the zoo, we'll go to a farm where we'll see a whale!")

Week Seven: Continue to remind you of the importance of you. And, maybe equally important, as repetitive as moments might seem and as much as you want to crawl out of your own skin, you better appreciate every single one of them.

I do. I really do.

COMMENTS:

Bernadette Z-S. This is a view I can relate to. Many a year I slept in the bottom bunk with my daughter Lauren in our apartment because she was afraid to go to sleep. It was my favorite time of day because that is when she began to share with me her joys and fears.

Pete K. Finally I get it. I'm a father of four beautiful girls, 2, 4, 6 and 8. After eight years, I've learned that there will always be laundry, dirty dishes and grass to cut. There will only ever be this one moment between me and my baby girl. Don't miss it. The rest of the world can wait. Like, my 8-year-old's birthday is today. She didn't even say goodbye going to school and now I'm caught grasping the last shadows of her childhood as she blurs into a young woman. Soak it up and cherish it. Your post today came at a perfect time.

Shannon L. I am at a similar place with my children. and you make me feel like life is perfect and where it needs to be.

WEEK EIGHT: My Bandwidth Is Full

I am looking for patience. It's a side effect of being eight weeks in.

Do I have patience with a baby who decides he doesn't want to eat at a normal feeding time? Yes. Patience with Parker's increasing boldness at testing boundaries? I'm remarkable. But patience with tedious adult tasks?

I've got nothing.

Like what happened when I dragged Parker and Hutch into a big-box store last week. Quick run-through to buy one thing. Parker was being a helpful big sister...until checkout. The Devil took over my little girl. She threw herself down screaming because I wouldn't buy her chocolate.

I paid, put the store bag on top of Hutch as he sat in his carrier, picked her up with the arm not carrying Hutch's seat, and carted us all off. I never let her see me bat an eye at her antics, though I did attempt an apologetic smile to those watching.

I find it odd that I can be fully patient with that mortifying, tedious drama from a tired toddler, but absolutely want to lose my mind when I can't find a parking space in a crowded lot. Or, when I go to use a coupon that expired the day before. Or, this was the worst, when I have to sit through a jury-duty video, which condescendingly explained the definition of *judge*.

Those are the things I used to laugh about.

Now they have the ability to unhinge me.

Here's my theory: For eight weeks, I've been so tolerant with indescribably stupid kid situations…so notably patient and understanding…I have nothing left for life's daily ups and downs. The parking spot, unusable coupon, and required video-watching become straws breaking this mama camel's back.

I know it'll get better. But right now, my bandwidth is full.

Once I get more sleep, get Hutch on a schedule, and time helps Parker mature…I should forego the errand if I can't find a parking spot, not care about the $2 coupon I can't use, and instead of getting frustrated by a video defining the word *judge* to a roomful of adults, shrug my shoulders, knowing some might need the basic lesson.

Another bit of even better news?

For every temper tantrum, there's a moment of sweetness.

As the weeks move on, there's no denying beautiful innocence—something this photo captured this week—is ultimately what sticks in my head and wins.

COMMENTS:

Emily C. I was behind you in Michaels last week and just smiled at what you were going through, because I know I will face that soon as a mom of a one-and-a-half-year-old...it makes you normal!

Maggie D. Even now with my third child in the 3-year-old range, I have yet to figure out why they say "Terrible Two's!" Those 2-year-olds don't hold a candle to a 3-year-old that has mastered how to use (mostly) words to express their anger and frustration all while laying in the floor screaming and kicking. Welcome to being a mom with someone no longer a toddler but not yet pre-K! Until we learn the secret on dealing, we can just keep propping each other up and giving knowing smiles and winks.

Teresa W. My story is from many years back but similar. As we ate a very nice dinner out, our 3-year-old decided to refrain from enjoying her food. We boxed hers up and as we left the restaurant, the antics began. Kicking and screaming..."They won't feed me!" That girl is now thirty-three years old and receives the same blessings from my beautiful grandchildren. Payback.

Tina A. I've told many people that age three was when my sweet child was possessed. It was like we woke up one morning and there was an announcer whispering: "Today, we have exchanged your adorable son with a honey badger on crack. Let's see if they can tell the difference!" As for the weird things that suddenly become completely and irrationally unbearable...I'm no help. I haven't figured that out yet.

WEEK NINE: Long Days = Short Years

Advent calendar is over halfway there, too many domestic responsibilities, and I'm asked to read *Where's Santa?*—modeled after
Where's Waldo?—every night as a bedtime story. That book will be
the death of me. This is page one of twelve.

Jam-smack in the middle of holiday traveling and hectic
Christmas everything…NOW is when sniffles turn into crusty
noses turn into hacking coughs turn into pediatrician appoint-
ments turn into nasal sprays, humidifiers, and fully sleepless
nights. Not just because one child is sick, but because both are.

It's annoying, but seasonal colds come and go. No reason to

make it sound dramatic. I only mention this because I'm mentally crafting what to say about Week Nine while rubbing Hutch's back, as I've been doing for an hour. He's too young to have most medicines, which means holding him is what makes him feel best. Sweet boy. He is such a sweet boy. That's what I keep whispering as he coughs on my shoulder. As for Parker, she can have medicine, but it takes eight times longer than necessary because she tries to negotiate M&M's as reward for taking it. She's definitely my daughter.

This time of year brings excitement, busy-ness and love.

It also opens my eyes to how fast kids grow. Development is at Mach 10.

Have you ever really thought about how children become a whole new person in one short year? Last year at two years old, Parker cried meeting Santa. This year she is totally into the storyline. She wants to rub Rudolph's nose and has opinions on how Elfie (our predictably-named Elf on the Shelf) must travel to the North Pole each night. A year ago, she wasn't evolved enough to have those thoughts. It's fascinating to now hear things drop out of her mouth like little clues about what's going on inside her head.

"Mommy, if reindeers eat carrots at each house, why don't they get full?"

"How come Santa comes down a chimney instead of walking in a front door?"

"How do they make ALL those toys?"

Hutch obviously has no clue about anything. Next year, I suppose, he'll be walking around tugging on Christmas tree branches. Two years from now, maybe he'll have enough mental capacity to stop his older sister from dressing him in girly reindeer booties. But for now, he's out of it. Just sits here and lets me rub his back.

I can't believe Parker is already three and a half, with a brain that questions whether we'll hear the reindeer when they land on the roof. I really can't believe butterball Hutch is nine weeks old, fitting in six-month-old clothing. Individual days can feel like an eternity, but a year-to-year comparison makes you think it's flying by.

Good thought to keep in mind during sick days, long nights, and this last stretch of Christmas crazy.

COMMENTS:

Jennifer L. I have days where motherhood is beating me up one side and down the other. Reading your posts makes me smile and feel as though I'm not nuts.

Cheryl H. Precious! Long days=short years.

 Molly. That's what I was trying to say, Cheryl. Long Days = Short Years. Would you mind if I changed the headline from "holidays" to this?

Mary R. Please keep posting. This Grandma reads them over and over.

WEEK TEN: True Love

It is undeniably breathtaking to see your three-year-old give an unsolicited kiss on her ten-week-old brother's head before merrily heading to the other room. Parker started it a couple of weeks ago. I don't know how or why. Sometimes she'll ask me to lean Hutch down when he's in my arms so she can kiss him. Other times she gives no announcement and needs no attention in return. It's pure and natural and one of the most tangible forms of love I've ever witnessed.

I write that as sincerely as I've written (complained?) about time management during newbornhood, or having to channel Pollyanna because Mary Poppins isn't coming.

But in this exact moment, on a grateful Christmas Eve, those things don't matter. Right now I can only think about my little human starting to actually feel more human. His neck is getting stronger. He smiles a ton more at both Wes and me.

But it's his connection with Parker that I'm fascinated to watch grow. She acts as if she didn't have three years of life without him. I see their love for each other despite both being too young to even know the definition of the word.

Amid the joy and holiday insanity, love is what it's all about.

Merry Christmas.

COMMENTS:

Tanya P. I finally realized today that I am not my six-month-old's favorite person. That honor belongs to his six-year-old brother. The sheer joy and love that shines through our baby whenever big brother walks in the room is amazing!

Herb L. Life would be heavenly, if we all loved like that.

Catherine P. My grandson was the same way when he turned 4 years old and his new sissy was born two weeks later. A bond that can't be broken. It's a BLESSING for them to have each other, too.

Tonya H. The love between siblings is miraculous.

WEEK ELEVEN: Tennessee Truck Stops

In the past eleven days, Parker and Hutch have ridden 1800 miles in the car. We've gone through six states. Charlotte to Kentucky, back to Charlotte, Christmas morning at home, repack, head to Florida, back to Charlotte, and then call it done.

I wasn't sure this was the smartest itinerary for two kids and a dog (Oh, did I forget that part? Yup. We also brought our dog. When I finally got around to calling the kennel to book his stay, it was full. So, joy of all joys, Fisher, our sixty-pound Wonderdog of a mutt, got thrown in the car too.), but I'm on maternity leave. I have the time off. Why not?

Here's why:

Because no matter how good a three-year-old and newborn are, if you force them to be in a car seat for multiple eight-hour one-way trips with minimal breaks, they are no longer themselves. Hell, I'm no longer myself.

In case you find yourself with a few miles to go, here are a few lessons learned in Week Eleven from traveling with a smart, chatty, inquisitive little girl and a constantly hungry baby boy.

- Goldfish crackers are as important as gas.
- Tennessee truck stops are not intended as family hangout centers.

- If you must use one as such, sit at a table near aisles of junk.
- Your three-year-old will assume every confederate-flag-painted and curse-word-shouting shot glass is a teacup for her doll.
- Don't remember diapers for babies but forget Pull-Ups for the older child.
- Avoid South Carolina's interstates. Two lanes on I-95.
- Calories consumed on car trips don't count.
- Little girls can hear Taylor Swift's "Shake It Off" on repeat for an hour. You might want to throw yourself out of the vehicle, but their happiness wins.

- Sitting between two car seats in the backseat holding a bottle to the mouth of a baby in one and trying to play sticker book with the other, with a big dog in your lap, does not make the trip go faster. It makes you wish for wine.
- Or a beach.
- Or one of those cartoon Jetson-mobiles that fly fast.
- If you keep the car moving—even at a snail's pace in traffic—it's an infant lullaby.
- That means driving on shoulder of the road isn't legal, but totally fine for you.
- If pulled over, just say you're toting around Romper Room. Roll down the back windows. Have the officer look inside. Kids will cry as if on cue.
- You won't get a ticket. The officer will walk away, grateful he's not you.
- Dream up car games. Lots of them.
- They can involve a window and the six words, "I spy with my little eye…"
- When you do get to your destination, you're allowed to expect family to greet you with open arms. They're so excited you're there! That's the fun part. They know the hassle you went through to come see them.
- Right? RIGHT???
- You're definitely allowed to be pissed when they aren't.

Most of all, when you are part of a circus confined to a car, act calm and happy. I'm serious. Even if the reality is that you want to jump off a cliff or switch into a new family, the more calm and happy you act, the more your kids will be the same. With every passing week I continue to find that both Parker and Hutch generally roll with what I throw their way—even if it's 1800 miles on the road.

COMMENTS:

David D. I'm a single male with no kids and I get pulled into your posts every time even though there is little chance I can relate.

Rebecca D. My five year old thinks shot glasses are what grown ups take medicine from…she's not wrong.

Jill C. Molly, once you have kids, the family comes to YOU. I just want to offer this advice. Have Christmas at home.

JANUARY

WEEK TWELVE: Going Back to Work

A certain amount of amnesia comes with newbornhood.

Tomorrow I go back to work full-tilt, anchoring four different shows. I'm ready. The past twelve weeks have been remarkable in their own way. I wouldn't change a second, except maybe lots of seconds I can't actually remember because I was pulling my hair out as they were happening.

Today I got reflective and went through photos. I look at this one taken exactly three months ago in the hospital bed, and have to wonder if I actually lived it—I can hardly recall what I'm seeing. It was taken Day One. Seeing it made me want to reread all previous eleven weeks.

I'm writing now after spending the past thirty minutes reviewing our past three months.

I'd forgotten lots. How freedom felt once I was cleared to drive again. The level of accomplishment I felt when Hutch crossed the twelve-pound mark. How difficult it was to feed him and give Parker a bath at the same time, then have neither want to go to sleep and both wake up at 3 a.m. How antsy I'd get on hour fourteen of a day with EVERY SECOND OF EVERY MINUTE SPENT with a three-year-old and a few-week-old.

But we got through it.

Now we're tossing up the routine again.

I don't worry about Hutch or Wes. Despite decades of age difference, they're both easygoing guys who let me set schedules and are into their own routines. Parker's a different ball game. Until three months ago, all she knew was that I worked evening newscasts and wasn't home weeknights. Now she's used to me putting her to bed. It's the best half hour of my day, and maybe hers too. It's just us. The two girls. She says that all the time.

"It's just us, Mommy. It's just girls."

Sometimes I stay beside her longer to watch her breathe as she sleeps. Her breath smells like SweeTarts. It swirls out of her nose and sits on her top lip. I like watching her eyes shut in a gentle way and hearing that sound of breathing. She'll sometimes instinctively—even in a dead sleep—reach for my hand. She feels me there. I stare and stare and stare. I love her so much and sometimes love her even more when she doesn't know I'm looking.

Starting Monday, it'll go back to how it was before—no time at night for "just us." We'll go back to our ritual of nighttime newsroom-to-bedroom FaceTime phone calls, where we blow kisses. Back to sitting separated to say bedtime prayers through a phone. On a really good evening, there'll be a quick break in my schedule where I can come home and hug her tightly. Now I'll also be hugging Hutch.

Maybe more of those extended-dinner-break nights will work out, but no matter how tomorrow and the night after that and the night after that and the many nights after that play out, they won't be like these past twelve weeks.

It's only a transition. Parker's an amazing little girl and will be okay. I know she feels loved, whether I'm there to tell her when tucking her into bed or in the morning when she wakes up. I'm not *worried* about her, I guess, but I am aware. Aware things will be different and aware she's gotten used to and likes the new way we've been doing things. As do I.

But because she's adaptable and awesome, and because I love my job and don't plan on changing it, I know we'll be just fine.

In looking back today, it became clear that one reason I'm grateful for work and happy to take this next step moving forward is because newbornhood has the ability to suck you dry. As much as I love my kids an indescribable amount, the past twelve weeks I dreamed of having time alone. I pined for it. I wanted nothing more than to have the ability to be in a space where no one needed me.

Never admitted that so directly and fully before now. Guess I was afraid it would make me sound like an ungrateful mother.

I've been a full-time mommy for twelve weeks. Now I'm going to go back to being full-time Molly. Not sure exactly how it'll work, adding the extra fifty-plus hours a week into my new two-kid schedule, but I know I cherish my children, am challenged by my job, and definitely want both. I feel confident it'll balance out.

COMMENTS:

Lauren H. I'm at week 13 with my baby, have an almost 2-year-old, and am going to work tomorrow too. I can completely relate to what you wrote here, and what you write each week and want to thank you. It's refreshing to know you're not alone at a time like this. There's someone else out there going through the same thing and having the same feelings.

Kristin S. Take a favorite night shirt of yours and make her a pillow from it. That way she always has a part of you at night. Good luck tomorrow!

Donna H. I so needed to read this tonight. You just have no idea. I start a job in a week after being a full time Mom for 7 years. I have been feeling so guilty about going back to work even with my kids being older. I think it's just the Mom in us. Good luck to you, Molly. And to me.

Alishia S. THANK YOU. Now I know I'm "normal."

Jumping In Fast

Busy first week. The cycle has begun.

Charlie Hebdo attacked. Hundreds of thousands across the world protest the terror in Paris and bring up questions about freedom of speech in democratic countries. A local military dad rides his bike 240 miles to raise money for his son. Severe fog in the mountains causes cars to tumble off the mountain. Separately, two North Carolina state troopers deliver a baby on the side of a road after an in-labor mom was in an accident. Two #MollysKids—kids I follow with uphill medical battles—go back into the hospital.

And, Antonio Sabato, Jr. randomly walked into the makeup room one afternoon as reporter Melissa Hankins (due next month!) and I were getting ready.

Back at it, baby.

It's exactly as I remembered.

FEBRUARY

MONTH FOUR: Hi.

Many of you have emailed and messaged about my weekly posts during maternity leave. I sincerely—very sincerely—thank you. I was unsure about writing them. Turns out the posts are my version of a digital scrapbook, only better because of your comments. I love them. Read every single one.

So, I'm here writing about my kids. I guess. Hi. Maternity leave feels like years ago.

Hutch just turned four months old. He weighs 17.5 pounds, has two teeth and wears nine-month-old clothing. I have serious fears

I'm raising a future linebacker. His roly-poly self is attached to the sweetest personality. He smiles lots and rarely cries.

Parker is as spitfire as ever. Clever, funny, and no matter what she's doing, she's in it to win it. She calls Hutch her own baby.

The adjustment going back to working fifty hours a week was more than I expected. Call me foolish, but I thought no beat would be skipped and it'd be just another transition. I was wrong.

In returning to work, Hutch was not the problem—in what can only be described as miracle timing, he started sleeping eleven hours straight the evening before I returned. I thought it was a fluke, but after four nights in a row, I thanked the angel who must be flying in to rub his back and keep him calm.

The problem, as predicted, is my mini-me. Parker—who never used to leave her room until "the sun is awake" and Hello Kitty's digital clock started with seven—now gets up every morning between 2 and 3 a.m. I'll pretend not to hear her bedroom door creak. She makes her way down the hall, walks up to my shoulder, taps it for sixty seconds, and starts to fake-cry. Her nightly excuses are always different. Always creative. Last night was "My pillow isn't comfortable."

Sometimes it's an effort to not laugh out loud.

This is a three-and-a-half-year-old's version of trying to understand why I'm no longer here at night. In her wickedly smart little mind, she's simply making sure I made it home. She wants to cling a little. I get that. Despite my exasperation at sleeplessness, I acknowledge her persistence as incredibly impressive.

What do I like about full immersion back at work?

Scheduling. Efficiency. I've been reminded that when time is tight, it forces a person to be productive. Not everything I want to get done has the space it might deserve. Tasks naturally bleed into one another.

For example, I've learned how to extend the use of a diaper because there are only four left and no time to get to a store for twenty-four hours. I've learned how to shower with Parker and Hutch (though I haven't yet figured how to shave with both there). Maybe most importantly, I've learned to adore early morning requests for a dance party, to play princess castle or color endless pages of *Frozen* activity books. I'm more happy to lie on my stomach with washable markers at 7:13 a.m. if I know I *can't* do it later.

This very real having-no-time-so-you-are-pyscho-productive-with-the-time-you-have rule also applies to non-kid situations. I walked into the newsroom the other day with those free disposable flip-flops you get at nail salons. I'd managed to squeeze in twenty minutes for an express pedicure. First one in months, and darn it, I needed those twenty minutes. I just didn't have the time to stick around and let it dry.

My boss pretended he didn't see my feet. My girlfriends laughed. Thirty minutes later, the heels were on. No harm, no foul.

You do what you do to get it all done, and get it done as well as you can.

This is Month Four. A Month Five post will be next. I've officially decided, as of one minute ago. The material is too fun not to write down.

COMMENTS:

Kelly Franson [former WBTV meteorologist]. Aww, miss those sweet (and sassy) kiddos! 1) This might be my favorite picture of Parker ever. 2) What on earth are you feeding that boy??? 3) Love you, Molls.

Frank W. You come into our living room each evening. Thanks for letting us into yours.

Debbie S. No one knows until they work a job that's not 9 a.m.-to-5 p.m. I used to go into work at 4:30 a.m. with a newborn and work split shifts so I could see my kids in the middle of the day, then go back to work. You do what you can with the time you have.

Kelly G. Thank goodness you are back to writing this! It's 4:56 a.m. and I've been up with my son since 2 a.m. teething and a cold! Your blog gives me joy!

I'm Back

While Parker was getting her third-ever "big-girl haircut" today, Miss Tiffany, got kinda serious.

Tiffany told me she needed to tell me something.

"I love your stories on Facebook," she said. "They sometimes break my heart, but I love them. And I love that you give big headlines with details and news stories that matter, because that's where I basically get all my news. My husband and I don't even watch the news anymore, I just get it from you on my phone. BUT"— imagine a squinty-eyed look of disdain—"BUT I need you to get back to posting pictures of the kids." She sounded stern. Like a direct order. "I loved your mommy blog. Why did you stop?"

OhMyGodIHateTheTerm *mommy blog.*

"I didn't stop! I went from writing weekly to writing monthly."

"But you've only written one since you were back at work from maternity leave," she said. "That was weeks ago. I'm sick of waiting."

"I—I'm going to write Month Five next week," I stammered. "Hutch turns five months old next week."

"Not good enough," she said. "I want *more.* Even if it's just thoughts when you have them, not a long post. Give me something. Give me a little bit. Or"—she flat-out sounded disgusted—

"at least you could post a couple pictures now and then."

At which point I took out my camera and snapped this photo, which made her laugh.

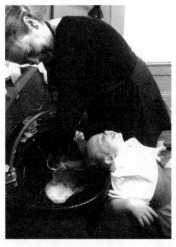

I've thought about what Tiff said all day. I really will write more about the kids. Or parenthood. Or the (sigh) "balance" of it all.

But can we please not call them "mommy blogs"? My ears hear that term and process it as a condescending statement said about a woman who *Oh! Isn't this so nice, has a little bit of time and wants to share a few thoughts about her day! And maybe after she shares her thoughts with her friends, they can all have tea and discuss drapery colors!*

That might be harsh, but that's how I think people—especially those who aren't stay-at-home parents—think of mommy blogs. It's not what they actually are. Not at all. There are *New York Times* bestselling authors with massive followings who write creative, brilliant mommy blogs almost every day. But I've heard the term get said with a dismissive tone—as though anyone could do them and they're not worth much. So, until that perception is universally changed, I'd rather not use the term.

Regardless of the words we use to describe what it is we're talking about, I do believe tons of us parents go through the same stuff all day long. And if what Miss Tiffany said is right, if reading about others' struggles and joys helps elicit camaraderie, then I should do it more. I'm sorry if anyone feels that I've left you hanging. That wasn't the intention. I was trying to not be TOO personal, because in the past I've always reported news stories, and didn't want to leave that behind.

But my mind is a melting pot of news, work, and life. Tiffany is right that maybe this page should reflect it all.

I'm back.

COMMENTS:

Bobbie H. Thanks, Tiffany, for expressing what a lot of us have been feeling!

Scott M. Another man chiming in—keep 'em coming. #PleaseAndThankYou

Pamela N. Wish I had thought of doing this 22 years ago when I had my son. Every once in a while I will read something you write and think…oh yeah…I remember that happening to my child. Thanks for taking us along for the journey and thanks for letting us relive some of those moments we had as our kids were growing up.

"You Hurt My Feelings."

Somebody along the way decided kids should learn more about feelings. Every cartoon, book, Disney Channel or Nick Jr. TV show—whatever outlet you're watching, reading, or hearing—either directly or indirectly teaches kids about feeling "sad," "scared," "confused," "angry," or "hurt." So-and-so is mean to someone. So-and-so is hiding beside a tree because they don't have friends. So-and-so is scared to talk to others in case those other kids aren't nice.

These are actual plot lines our children absorb every day.

I am over it.

Here's one of many reasons why: Parker looked at me today when I calmly told her no in response to having a second pretzel M&M. I said it in a normal voice I've used a hundred times before, and she looked at me, folded her arms over her chest, put her head down, and started to whine.

Whatever. She's a kid. No problem.

Then she got louder. When I told her to please act like a big girl, she replied through dramatic gulps of air, "You, you, you, you... [gulp]...you hurt my feelings!"

Excuse me?

My fearless, independent, and opinionated little girl thinks that by pouting about "hurt feelings," she'll sucker me into giving her what she wants? I get being almost four, having temper tantrums, and testing boundaries. But when did limiting the number of M&M's become hurtful to her psychological state?

Go back to paragraph one. That's your answer. She doesn't even watch that much TV, and "hurt feelings" are what she takes away from the little that she does see.

Furthermore (my soapbox is getting wider), why do young kids need to be taught about hurt feelings? Won't unpleasant feelings naturally emerge in due time? Why is "so-and-so doesn't have any friends so they're sad" even a THING in cartoons for pre-kindergartners?

I'm not a childhood expert. I'm just a woman. A parent. A person who believes kids can figure this out on their own. If someone makes them mad, they can react or cry or push back or talk with an adult at that time. We can encourage them to do so and should teach them that we're here to listen.

But are we teaching them to be ultrasensitive?

And if we are, why?

After the M&M moment, Parker asked if I'd read her a book. Of course. I asked her to pick one out.

She returned with, *Today I Feel Silly and Other MOODS that Make My Day.*

Hello, attorney. Here is your evidence for the jury of Me.

Exhibit A (Page 5): "My friends had a play date. They left me out. My feelings are hurt. I want to shout!"

Exhibit B (Page 21): "Today I'm discouraged and frustrated— see? I tried Rollerblading and fell on my knee."

Exhibit C (Page 23): "Today I am sad, my mood's heavy and gray. There's a frown on my face and it's been there all day."

I'm 100,000% on board with teaching Parker to be selfless and aware of others, but by reading this book I think I just taught loneliness, anger, and heavy moods.

Feelings are good. Feelings can be expressed. But she's three. Come on.

COMMENTS:

Jennifer H. YES!! I agree! Thank you for saying this...I was wondering if I was the only one rolling my eyes at these things.

Britt Y. Preach it. We are creating monsters with all this feeling talk. Feelings are an important indicator that we can use to direct/change behavior. OUR OWN behavior. Let's please stop giving them life as a tool to manipulate other people and situations.

Mary H. A wonderful way for children to learn about feelings is to be taught to care for the feelings of others.

Lilian W. It could be seen many different ways. Some kids need to learn that their feelings are ok, and everyone has them.

Leigh L. I retired from teaching 3 year olds in May after twenty-three years and the times have really changed. Now when my almost 4-year-old granddaughter says you hurt my feelings whenever we say no, we just tell her that's too bad but when you are rude you hurt our feelings. She doesn't get it really but we aren't jumping through hoops just because she isn't happy. I really saw parents change in the years I taught preschool—and not for the better.

Barbara E. From a parent of a 16-year-old child with autism who only recognizes three emotions (happy, sad, and angry) in himself and others, I sometimes wish these books and TV shows were around as such when he was much younger. It's terrible to watch him struggle with his own emotions and trying to recognize them in others. I'm not saying this is right for everyone, it's just my point of view. Embrace Parker's recognition of others' feelings, and her own. Not all kids have that ability!

MARCH

Makeup

Childcare got sticky. No pre-school. Wes is traveling. A neighbor could sit with Hutch but not watch a rambunctious Parker. So I did what I had to do and took her to work with me. And I'm worried, because who brings a three-year-old to a corporate, fast-paced setting in the middle of a busy day?

Only...she's awesome and loves it. LOVES it. Is on her BEST behavior. Colored beside me with her washable paint markers as I sat in a meeting, then quietly toted her artwork to a nonglamourous changing room to watch me put on makeup.

Before I even drew the correlation she said aloud:

"Mommy, you're painting your face and I'm painting my book!"

COMMENTS:

Kelly J. You took your girl to work. Your bosses didn't scream. I have a whole new respect for WBTV.

Sara H. Some jobs don't care. They expect you to be there whether or not you have a babysitter for you kids. That is a great mother daughter day.

Sarah H. More workplaces need childcare! Gotta do whatcha gotta do as a mama.

Nichole S. I'm thinking you may be the victim…a sucker for a cute smile and an awesome compliment.

MONTH FIVE: Connections

I love that right here, right now, I can pound out thoughts about a five-month-old boy and an almost-four-year-old girl and the way they love each other and the magical way he makes her seem like she's almost-four going on fourteen.

A moment just happened. Hutch and I were just hanging out. One of those special times you appreciate sitting with your baby. I'd spent ten minutes raising my voice an octave, tickling Hutch's tummy, eating his toes and doing all the things I could think to make my bowl-of-jelly boy smile. He looked back at me stone-faced, like I was crazy. Which I might be. But then Parker walked in with a calm air that screamed, *Let me show you how this is done.* Without saying a word, she put her face up in his nose and said…nothing. She just stared.

With virtually no effort, he smiled.

Just to rub it in, she also made him sweetly coo.

They have a connection.

I love it so much.

This Tuesday marks Month Five. Hutch is cruising along. He now wolfs down baby food, rolls over during tummy time, continues to sleep like a dream, and adores being outside. Nothing makes him smile more than his sister Parker and fresh air. He's great.

But bliss is not constant, and every parent has a breaking point. Mine was physical. It happened two Fridays ago.

I was on my twelfth day of work in a row. The industry is tough like that because news happens 365 days a year. Headlines happen on holidays and really intense times—terror attacks, severe weather, special reports, etc.—can put a strain on the entire staff. Producers work their tails off, editors are called in, reporters and photographers do double shifts, and anchors set up shop on-set day after day after day. It calibrates itself later in slower moments, and schedules can be adjusted to give time back to hardworking employees. Most of us understand because we got into this field as fast-paced people who want to be where the action is, but we're also all only human. It can take a toll.

These past few work weeks have been hectic because our

newsroom was preparing special reports for an upcoming "ratings month." Most newsrooms will tell you ratings matter every day. Honest newsrooms will also say those ratings matter even more a specific few months out of the year. February is one of them. When I came back from maternity leave, it was to immediately prepare for this ratings month (also casually referred to as "sweeps"). This was expected and no problem. What was unexpected was that Wes started traveling more for work. Our logistics were forced to become an even more well-oiled machine that ran on Post-it notes, texts about timing, double childcare, and lots of understanding.

We were spinning through relatively unscathed *until* Parker got sick. It was after dinner. I was at work. She was at home throwing up for the first time in her life (that she could remember), and scared to death about what was happening to her body.

She wanted to call after each bout. I'd be working on a script, see my phone ring, pick up, and hear the most pathetic little voice: "Mommy, my tummy hurts."

I left the 11 p.m. show in the second commercial break after we were through with the news and weather. It was ostensibly to get home to her, but also because I, too, felt terrible.

I'll spare you the graphic details. We've all been there and know what it's like. Needless to say, Parker and I spent the night in my bed with one of us waking every half hour to hopefully make it to the bathroom in time. At one point my sweet girl fell back asleep, clinging to a mixing bowl in the bed with us while wrapping her other arm around my neck.

It was disgusting and awful and stinky

and

human and loving and remarkably comforting.

Though we had a big Saturday planned, I was too weak to make mental decisions and instead let all balls being juggled fall with a thud. Best part? I didn't care. Lying in bed with my little girl, sipping Sprite, watching horrible cartoons and staying away from the rest of the world was the only thing that mattered.

Parker was in sick-girl heaven. Which made my heart happy, despite my stomach, which felt like I was on a boat in a hurricane. The worst twenty-four hours in a very long time showcased how nasty things sometimes have the best silver linings.

I learned a few more lessons in Month Five, too. (Like I said, it has been busy.) If you go for a walk with kids on bikes, don't go too far one way. You must return, and carrying a bike on top of a stroller filled with two children is a nightmare. Also, if you're too lazy and just plain tired to get everyone dressed on Saturday, declare it "Pajama Day." Microwave pancakes work for any meal.

This month, I also had a strange sense of pride hearing Parker order the boys around on her new soccer team. She'd yell, "You aren't supposed to use your hands! Only use your feet!"

Oddly, watching her order other girls around in ballet class made me want to apologize to their moms.

Also, losing an hour for daylight savings impacts a baby's day; introducing pureed food SERIOUSLY alters the diapers you're changing; when teaching the alphabet it's easy for a child to mix up *C* and *S*, but they'll somehow know *P* stands for *princess*, *Q* for *queen*, and *E* for *Elsa*; and loving babysitters are precious people in life, not to be taken for granted.

Here's to all who take care of a child with the flu, sometimes drop balls, and are breathlessly in love with watching magical connections grow.

COMMENTS:

Dana A. Right there with ya! It gets hairy sometimes but it's also pretty sweet.

Patricia H. What a good girl to hug your neck as she sleeps.

Mary V. Ok so there is no way Hutch is turning five months already! I must be too busy! Toddlers are the answer to time travel because you simply can't keep up!

Nicholas M. I enjoy escaping into your reality through your words.

Fran W. These descriptions are priceless.

Nadja M. Your children will grow to understand your sense of humor.

Hutch Has a Helmet!

They actually call them "medical headbands." That's a PR thing. "Headband" sounds cuter than "helmet." But I call things what they are: my boy has a helmet. A pretty darn adorable one. We got it Thursday. He wore a onesie to embrace the concept.

Different children need these for different reasons. Hutch needs it because the right back side of his head is misshapen.

Measurements show it's pretty severely misshapen, and his ears and cheeks were starting to not be symmetrical. He's healthy and happy and still a joy—I am not worried about this addition to his life in the slightest—we just need to mold him into a better shape.

I'm going to use this post to educate all those who know nothing about helmets for babies. I knew nothing. Had I seen one on a child, I'd have assumed there was something drastically wrong.

That doesn't have to be the case. Hutch is 100% healthy.

Five months old is a good age to get one because the skull is really malleable. Hutch will wear his twenty-one to twenty-four hours a day for up to twelve weeks. He'll take it off for bath time, pools, etc. After that, we remeasure and see if another helmet is needed. The helmets are custom-made, so pressure is put on particular points for each child where pressure is most needed.

Though the helmet looks a little clunky, it doesn't hurt. Tons of kids have them. In fact, one doctor told me Charlotte has more kids wearing these types of helmets than any city in America.

Really?

I'm not sure if that's because the marketing departments are better here or because there's actual real need. I can only speak for Hutch. And believe me, his sweet head needs this bad boy. They supposedly work wonders. We're going to get him all shaped up.

Also, you can get the helmets painted.

I'm told there's a woman in Lincoln County who does a heck of a job. I already have a design in mind…

COMMENTS:

Beth M. He is adorable! And a DeAngelo Williams helmet would look great on him.

 Molly. Love that idea. But it's not my design thought…

Lauryn F. My boy just got his taken off a few days ago! Babies are so resilient…it didn't seem to bother him one bit. I have actually missed it this weekend as he's bumped his head quite a few times.

Teri M. Here's my little fighter pilot!

Kim T. Abby graduated from her D.O.C band three weeks early because we made sure she wore it, never missed an appointment, and always did her stretching.

Cari O. Our little guy just finished last week! He had to have two bands.

Rob K. This was our first day with ours. I strapped on a bike helmet to match for the first couple hours while we played. Three months later it was off.

Linsay K. I wore one 20 years ago. Best of luck to Hutch! Can't wait to see the design.

Introducing…"The Incredible Hutch"

All I told Leigh Gibson, a woman who paints baby helmets out of her own home, was "green with Hulk-like font." Two hours later she came back with this freestyle amazingness that even had a happy looking Hulk-baby.

Thank you to EVERYONE who sent pictures of their own children wearing "headbands" after I wrote about Hutch joining your club. What an education. I've seen designs from local artists, sibling-decorated ones with stickers, and moms and dads who put sports team decals on their babies' bands. How rewarding to see and read your success stories.

Thank you.

COMMENTS:

 Molly. This is Leigh.

Karen H. Leigh is awesome! She painted my son's as well.

Krysten J. My son was born with plagio (like Hutch) so we saw Leigh when he was 5 months old. All I told her was I wanted, "I do my own stunts" on the front and I wanted it to be fox racing. She came up with the design. Good luck on your helmet journey Hutch!

APRIL

The Horror of Hutch's White Wicker Basket

Hutch looks particularly happy here during a recent hour-long helmet break.

Cute outfit, right?

Do not always believe what you see. Pictures show what's on the surface, not the whole story. Photo shoots, Christmas cards, Facebook, and Instagram can all look perfect but actually be hiding the truth. That's the case here with Hutch's outfit.

It begins with his closet. Actually, *closet* is a stretch. His *actual* closet is filled with junk, leaving no room for baby clothes. So Hutch's clothes are in an overstuffed white wicker basket kept with no rhyme, reason, or organization. I refer to this basket as his *closet*.

I tackle lots of things head-on, but admit that when it comes to keeping up with Hutch's wardrobe, I am not only not tackling it, I'm walking off the field, refusing to even participate in the game.

I don't know if it's because he's a boy and boy clothes aren't as cute, or if it's because he changes sizes on an almost weekly basis. But in almost six months of his life, I've only bought one new outfit for him—a "Little Brother" onesie at a checkout line in a grocery store. That's it. (And yes, a grocery store checkout.)

Suffice it to say that Hutch is king of the hand-me-downs, because my brother Jay and his wife Amy send us all their little boy's clothes. In return, I send Parker's old clothes to their little girl. Great system. We are all saving tons of money.

However, these unmarked massive boxes of clothes mean I have no idea what Hutch has available to wear. I've dumped the contents of them into his wicker basket, without sifting through. It just seems too overwhelming to sort. The sizes are all so similar, yet different. Maybe some parents would look at this as a fun project; I look at it as an unnecessary one. He'll wear what he'll wear and so be it.

Every morning, sometimes twice a day, I blindly rifle through that wicker basket. Every size and season together, from newborn to eighteen months. It's like sticking your hand into a barrel of candy with your eyes squeezed shut, having no idea what goodie you'll grab. You just pull it back out and hope you like that flavor. (This is in comparison to Parker's neat, almost OCD looking closet, where every dress hangs straight and even the tights are in some semblance of color-coded order. I can't explain it.)

When I remove my hand from Hutch's basket, I hope it holds something that A) fits, and B) doesn't have some cartoon character on it whose name I don't know. The other day my hand removed a pair of baby jeans. Quick glance at the label: *12 months*. Hutch is only five months, but built like a refrigerator. I assumed they would work.

I had to HEAVE to pull the jeans over his adorable fat rolls. He's big, but why did twelve-month-old-size jeans barely get up over his lower legs? I didn't get it. At one point I almost pulled Hutch off the changing table, yanking and yanking and yanking upward. Calm boy didn't cry one bit. He actually seemed to be smiling at my frustration. This took me five minutes—FIVE MINUTES!—to get the denim over his knees to the bottom of his diaper, that I realized at that exact moment, had just been filled.

Maybe that's why he was smiling.

Did I remove those jeans to change the diaper? No, sir-ee. Not on your life. We were 60% of the way toward our goal and I wasn't about to go back to ground zero. I dropped them just down enough—maybe 10% more—to get to his diaper successfully. Once wiped, dried, powdered, and hand sanitized, it was back to pushing, pulling, and yanking.

The thighs were obstacles unto themselves. The jeans just didn't want to go. He wiggled, as if to help this disastrous mothering attempt. Finally—finally—success. Oddly enough, once up to his waist, they buttoned easily.

When I lifted him up, I saw the tag was sticking out the back.

Before tucking it in, I saw the fine print underneath the size:

Skinny Jeans.

Oh my God.

WHO MAKES SKINNY JEANS FOR A BABY?

Furthermore, WHO MAKES SKINNY JEANS FOR A BABY BOY??

I was seething and mad at society, Baby Gap, and everyone in the fashion industry. Then the most outrageous question of all popped in my head.

WHY DO I HAVE THESE FOR HUTCH AND NOT KNOW IT???

That one's my fault.

I added *deal with white wicker basket* to the mental to-do.

Sure hope after I cut these jeans off him and get to bath time—the next moment I reach around for something to wear—I pull out a pair of pajamas with a zipper, and not those dang buttons along the legs.

COMMENTS:

Lyndsey S. Cut yourself a break. I'm laughing with you, not at you.

Kimberley P. I know this was just a post in between the months, but I liked it so much and am laughing so hard I'm already waiting for Month Six.

Russ M. You got me to read about kid clothing.

MONTH SIX: Stroller Talks

Hutch turned six months yesterday. He really is Incredible. I can't take credit; some babies are just born this way. He sleeps well, laughs a lot, doesn't cry often, lets me drag him on countless errands, and has cheeks that I can't stop kissing. The best part about him, however, is that he LISTENS to his sister.

Parker's new favorite thing is to sit on the handlebars of his stroller and tell him stories in dramatic fashion. I wish I had every conversation on tape.

He stares up at her never once interrupting. He watches her face intently. She can be talking about pumpkin Cinderella coaches, or, out of nowhere, like last night when I snapped this photo, coconut trees.

My girl loves an audience, even if it's a six-month-old who can't respond. At some point in the midst of a never-ending imaginative tale, he'll reach his arm out and grab at her messy, hippie-flowing hair. She takes it as a sign that he's fully engaged and keeps talking.

If this is what having a six-month-old and four-year-old means, sign me up. I'm locked in.

COMMENTS:

Jeannette G. It all takes energy. From you and them. Sometimes short entries can be the best.

Sherry S. My children are grown but your blogs remind me of moments in my own kid's lives and how much I wanted perfection only to fail miserably. If only I'd gone for quality time instead of worrying about what others would think.

Heather V. I am teary-eyed. The vividness of those tedious times fade and go from the mind quicky. Unless, I guess, you write it all down...

MAY

Mornings and Meltdowns

Some days by 9:20 a.m., I feel like I could go back to bed. The day should just be over.

There was a time not so long ago when I'd wake whenever I woke, stretch, and casually get coffee. Because working the 11 p.m. news makes for late nights, mornings were relax-time.

Mornings are now a machine.

As soon as the digital clock beside Parker's bed has a 7 in the beginning—she's gotten over her middle-of-the-night hall walks and the 7 is her sign that she can leave her room—it's on. She's out of there, heading down the hall directly to my shoulder. She stands beside my prone body, taps me repeatedly, and announces everything in her head. Within sixty seconds we are walking to get Hutch, who generally just waits for someone to acknowledge him.

Then it's breakfast, bottles, clean-up, clothes, and whatever entertainment ensues. (We had a dance party at 8 a.m. today to *The Little Mermaid*'s "Under the Sea." I was still on my first cup of coffee.) On mornings there's preschool, I box lunches, brush hair, belt kids in car seats, mentally plan/pack what's needed for errands with Hutch after preschool drop-off, and back down the driveway. The whole thing is ridiculously exhausting. My mind isn't a mind: it's one big list.

I bow down to my friends who have to add in pickups and carpools and homework and instruments.

If the robot-like routine is on schedule and both children are content in the car as we leave, I'm euphoric. I've carted around one child for four years and two kids for almost seven months, yet I still find it fist-pump gratifying to successfully accomplish the first 120 minutes of every day.

But, if the kids are unnecessarily whiny, I just want to crawl back into bed.

It was the latter two days ago.

I was overly ambitious in trying to head to the grocery BEFORE preschool drop-off. The day was going to be completely packed with no other time for this task, food was needed, whatever, whatever, whatever. I'm chastising myself now. It was a dumb call. But in my mind, we'd just be running in…

If you've never gone to the store with multiple kids and a list, enjoy the absence of this life experience. It's not efficient, easy, or enjoyable.

Hutch's car seat fits on top of the front handle of the grocery cart. Parker insists on either A) riding in the cart with arms in airplane position, à la Leonardo DiCaprio and Kate Winslet in *Titanic* or B) curling up in fetal position on the bottom rack so she's low to the ground "in a princess fort."

Both options are awful. Both options are also better than option C) walking beside me with full access to every item.

Any parent will tell you taking kids to a grocery store can absolutely be done. You just need patience and time.

Patience and time were not on my side two mornings ago. Nor was luck.

For the first time ever in the history of Hutch's life, he had a meltdown in public.

It was a doozy. I'm shuddering as I recall it right now. All the crying he never does was bottled up so tight, the cork suddenly popped. The unexpected, continual wail sounded like loud squeals mixed with pain. Stop-in-your-tracks-whip-your-head-around, "What's-that-terrible-mother-doing-to-her-child??!?!" type of noises. This happened in the checkout line.

Sole lane open. Trapped. One person ahead and one person behind.

Now I ask you—if you successfully have everything on the list in the cart, are minutes from loading items on the conveyor belt, and the finish line is in sight—do you surrender? No matter how badly your child is screaming?

No way.

I apologized to every shopper there. You know who you are. I also gave a deep level of thanks to the kind lady with loving eyes who offered help. She was a great-grandmother sitting on the bench waiting for her family to walk through the store. Her cane and bad knee wouldn't permit her to carry the baby, she said, but she could make faces at him to try to keep him quiet while I paid.

It didn't work, but her efforts were appreciated.

I've never bagged groceries so fast in my life. Bread smushed by heavy cans. Overstuffing some bags, too few things in others. Couldn't've cared less. *Just get us out of there.*

Once in the sunshine, Hutch stopped crying. Of course. He just wanted to head the heck home.

Two days later, now I see the humor. Especially when I remember what Parker asked in the height of the crisis:

"Mommy, what's wrong with Hutch?"

Without thinking, without even looking up from bagging, I'd replied quickly.

"He's practicing his singing voice. Do you like it?"

I don't know where that answer came from, but she didn't follow up and I was grateful for her silence.

She was quiet (I now realize) because she was listening to Hutch's voice. Like, actually trying to form an opinion on his talent. Once we were finally on the road and he fell asleep, she said:

"Mommy, Hutch doesn't sing very nicely. I hope he never sings again."

You and me both.

COMMENTS:

Tracy H. Parker's humor. A silver lining in otherwise dark cloud.

Sylvia H. Every mother has had to endure the screaming child in the check-out line!

Marty S. Sorry to say that I am DYING LAUGHING.

Roland S. Bless your heart!

Cathy B. You made my day. Took my two babies shopping today. I couldn't wait to get home.

MONTH SEVEN: Teaching a Sense of Self

Hutch hit 7 months old on the same day I tacked on another year.

What I thought about me:

Oh. Another birthday.

What I thought about him:

He appears to have cheek implants.

I love when he opens his mouth and shows off four sharp teeth.

He looks like a happy saber-4-toothed tiger when he laughs at his own noise.

He never stops eating.

He started nibbles of human food—roast beef, zucchini, pasta, red peppers, even onions.

As long as he's fed, he's incredibly chill.

His fat rolls.

I love them.

Especially around his ankles.

I'm grateful his helmet is working.

I'm ready for his helmet to be off.

He has now discovered all body parts. Bath time is interesting.

He claps! All the time!

Hand-to-mouth: chews on computer plugs, shoes, necklaces, the dog's ear, dish towels, my fingers, fuzzy living room shag carpet lint, his toes, stuffed animals, and (oops) markers.

Why on my birthday do I have zero thoughts about me, and a list I could type forever about him?

Because your children naturally take up way more space in your head than your own self.

But on this Sunday night after a long week, I'm going to admit that thinking about them all the time is also tiring.

The simplicity wears me out in an exhausting way. It's not hard exhausting. It's mundane exhausting. Make sure everyone is fed. Clean. Playing. Having fun. Then time to feed again. Stay clean. Let's play and have fun. Feed. Clean up. Have fun.

The details change; every day is different. But the general order seems pretty strict.

Wait. Having déjà vu. Didn't I write about this during maternity leave? Wasn't I exhausted by the routine in one of those early weeks? I distinctly remember the "Nap. Feed. Play." structure wearing me down. I'm having the same sensation again right now, six months later.

Does anything ever change?

I think it does. A big difference now is that though it remains exhausting, it's not boring. Watching a five-week-old do nothing most of the time could get boring. Nothing in today's life is boring—four-year-olds impress and a seven-month-old clapping makes me smile—but constant kid conversations at home are filling my head and making my list of adult things I personally value very, very short.

So yes, it's GREAT I can instantly think of two hundred things to tell you about Hutch, but on my own birthday I need to have something else in my head. Right? Something about me and what I love and who I am. Right? Otherwise I'm selling myself short. Right?

Right.

My kids shouldn't define me.

My brilliant girlfriend Melissa (the one who was pregnant in the makeup room when Antonio Sabato, Jr. walked in) said the other day about her now-four-month-old little girl, "I think one of the best lessons I can give is to make sure she sees me living life."

Those words resonated. Melissa loves her daughter. Period. But the truth of the matter is that Melissa could give her daughter no better lesson than just being Melissa and never losing the many things that make her an amazing woman. Her daughter is lucky to have Melissa to watch...so let her watch.

Let her be inspired.

Melissa shouldn't—and isn't—going to lose her own self just because she's carrying a diaper bag.

Confession: I just took a break from writing this to feed Parker and Hutch, give them baths, put him to bed, and get her started on a minuscule 646-piece Lego Disney Princess castle project. So believe me, I'm fully aware of how kids take precedence.

But I'm still on board with carving out time to be YOU.

Be it kid-free with friends, getting into hobbies, playing golf, watching sports, singing, dancing, reading, working out, painting furniture, writing, meditating, practicing archery, cooking for fun, hot-gluing corks on vintage frames—whatever!—we have to find time for us.

Parker is ten feet away with her 646 pieces. I'm on the computer, writing. She's being her. I'm being me. I told her that Mommy was temporarily closed because she needed quiet time. Parker is fiddling with small plastic Legos, but also watching me closely. She's absorbing me taking time for me. I'm good with that.

I feel like many of us live life in the far-left lane twenty-four hours a day, speeding through life. We can't always remember the exits we just passed. For me, there are two car seats in the back. They help make the vehicle full and add lots of incredible stops and future extra destinations. But it's still my car. I'm still driving. And though my car seats dictate where to go at times, I want the two kids in those seats to grow up as self-aware when they're at the wheel, because they watched someone who figured out directions on her own.

"Me" time is now up. Lego castle finished. Off to put a four-year-old to bed.

COMMENTS:

Rob E. Your posts are a wonderful reminder (for me) of bygone days. Our children are 29, 26, 21 and 19. The "nest" is empty. And, yes, we had 10 consecutive years of diapers, and chattering, and Barney, and emergency room visits: stitches, multiple broken arms, a broken leg, a concussion AND a bead or two up a nose. Please save these for your kids. They'll love reading them in about 15 years.

Kelly L. I have only one true regret in life. And that is never having had the chance to be a mom. I don't let myself think about it much; it's not something I dwell on. But every once in a while something really hits me that I've missed out on the greatest blessing. I know it might sound odd Molly, but I get to live a little through the real stuff of child-raising with you.

 Molly. I've watched you talk to kids with pediatric cancer, based on your own journey. You're an inspiration to many.

April M. So true. We are not just mommies.

Ginger H. I recently had the same realization. I do need time for me and I need to not feel guilty about it. But it is hard.

Nicole T. Amen sister.

Wendy B. I have a 3 1/2 year old boy and 2 month old little girl. I feel like we are living parallel lives, as I often say and think what you write.

JUNE

MONTH EIGHT: Mental Snapshots

Hutch added a new food group to his diet this week: sand.

He must be the only child on the face of the earth who not only likes to eat sand, but LOVES to eat sand. He loves sand more than any food he has ever tried, which is saying a lot. (Parker nicknamed him "the Refrigerator" for a reason.)

At first I worried. Would he choke on small shells? Is sand digestible? I did a finger sweep of his mouth and pulled out wet hunks. Instead of being grateful the gritty grains were gone, he went berserk. He was flat-out pissed I'd taken away his new delicacy.

I quickly put some back in.

If Hutch doesn't care that sand is up his nose and in his eyes and ears, I don't. If he's happy (and quiet) shoveling fistfuls in his mouth, then I shall be happy and quiet too. The sand makes nightmarish diapers, but it's a small price to pay for a content beach baby.

So go for it, Hutch-buddy. Act like your nickname. You've got a whole beach in front of you.

Plus, Hutch eating sand gives me time to build a castle with Parker, and answer her 8,935,679 questions on anything within eyesight.

Tomorrow marks eight months. Feels every single bit like eight long months.

The number-one thing people say to moms with young kids is: "Time flies! Enjoy them while they're this age." I hear that at least once a day; it must be true. But if you are the parent at the beach watching your baby eat sand and having your ears constantly needed by your four-year-old, the "enjoying" part sometimes gets lost.

I try to write with utter honesty. Therefore, I say this:

Moments can be hard to appreciate when you're in the midst of living them.

⊂ȝ℘

There are pockets this week at Kure that I've desperately wished for just ONE unattainable hour where I don't need to worry about the kids. Even if Wes takes them, there's inevitably an escaped Parker running to cry for me soon into my "break," or Hutch is pooping out sand and only I know where the diaper cream is located. I want sixty minutes where I can take a chair to the water's edge. Keep my toes dug in where every third wave washes them. Get tan. Read a whole book in one afternoon. Be on the beach for ten hours straight.

You know, do what I used to do. Pre-kids.

Then my mind hears many voices say, "Time flies! Enjoy them while they're this age."

As annoying as that statement is to hear, it has made me—I've actually found myself consciously doing this—take a mental snapshot. I hope this doesn't sound cheesy because I'm ACTUALLY doing this and it's ACTUALLY working.

Take Hutch and sand.

Just as I was about to scream with frustration earlier today, I stopped myself. I stopped everything. I told myself, "*Don't scream*." I *made* myself think, "They won't always be this age." I closed my eyes, counted backward from five (only five because there's no telling what Hutch could have in his mouth if I gave him ten), reopened them, and actually *looked* at what was in front of me.

When I opened them I saw the same messy disaster of a baby chomping on sand with his seven teeth.

But I also saw something else. I saw an incredibly happy child. I saw an eight-month-old well on his way to loving the beach as much as his mom does.

The exact thing that had been stressing me out five seconds before was suddenly enjoyable.

It also spurred me to grab my phone and make my mental snapshot a real one.

Right after I took this picture, Hutch opened his mouth to smile. Sand tumbled down. He made a noise that sounded like his laugh, only garbled and thick. Which made me laugh. Which calmed me more.

And then—because she hadn't ever stopped chatting—Parker, who was beside us, asked Question Number 8,935,680: "Mommy, why do seagulls fly instead of ride on boats?"

A minute before I would've been irritated at her incessant chatter. Now, I simply answered.

"Because they have wings. If you had wings, you'd want to fly all the time too."

Stopping to really SEE in front of me made me not only appreciate, but adore her four-year-old questions and pervasive creativity. It reminded me of how much I love her mind. It reminded me exactly of where she got her demanding persistence in always wanting answers.

So there we sat, Hutch shoveling sand into his mouth and Parker dreaming up storylines for the princesses she was inviting to live in the castle we'd built.

It almost, for a moment, felt easy.

CB80

I know this beach trip is not like past ones. I pine for the ocean I know in my soul, where the music of waves is never interrupted by cartoons in the other room. The insane pace I drive of go-go-go stops—it lifts when I smell salt water. The beach is the only place in the world I've ever been able to really let other responsibilities go. I can relax at the ocean. I don't care about my phone.

Only, this trip has made me well aware the words *relax* and *babies on vacation* don't exactly go together.

But you know what? There is peace here. It's just not as obvious. It only came to me today after stopping a moment to take in the chewing sand and chirping voices.

I'm finding a whole new beauty in my already breathtaking view.

I'm sure everyone is right—this time will go fast. Probably too soon the chair will once again be by the water's edge, toes will be in the sand, and a book will be read for fun.

I wonder if then it'll be this week I'm reliving? Maybe I'll be laid back in that chair, recalling mental snapshots of a roly-poly baby and a sweet little girl who looks to me for all her answers.

COMMENTS:

Hannah R. The mental snapshot is not cheesy at all. It's beautiful.

Amy L. Love, love, love this. Thank you. This might just be what saves my sanity next week as I take my three to the beach, one being 18 months. I've been so worried about how stressful the trip will be instead of relaxing.

 Molly: It's wonderful, amazing, and not relaxing one bit.

Nicole S. Tip for you- rubbing baby powder on their skin takes the sand right off—it's GREAT for those diaper changes on the beach.

Kristen A. Here in Holden Beach this week with my 8-month-old Sand Monster. Glad he's not the only one with a sand obsession! This is me attempting to corral the sand-eating. I think I should give up.

Wendy P. All three of my babies loved sand. I have pictures of me offering them food and they only wanted the sand.

Sherry K. Made me long for last October when my son and his then 14-month-old son and 4-year-old daughter made their first trip to the Atlantic Ocean with me all the way from Utah. I will never forget that week at Bald Head Island with my baby and his own babies. It's a reminder of what really makes life precious.

Ginger H. My son, Hudson (10 months), LOVES sand! When I held his hands so he couldn't get any, he'd just bend & put his face in the sand to get some! I couldn't believe it! Now he loves to eat dirt of any kind, he doesn't discriminate! I'm scared he's going to end up on an episode of "My Strange Addiction!"

Julie K. Our family has the same feelings about the beach. My oldest crawled INTO the ocean constantly like a sea turtle. My youngest built endless sand castles with his too short time with his late Pop Pop. The beach is totally my relax place.

Marchalle C. And the day will come when they will meet you at the beach and leave before you do! And you will watch that mom with the young kids and smile remembering when! A truth from the blog of my heart.

Beverly D. Before you know it, you will be my age (60+), retired, living at the beach five months out of the year…waiting for your grandchildren to join you for their vacation with Happy Antici-pation…because I can finally sit at the water's edge with my toes dug into the sand for hours on end…but ALONE! No chatter, no diapers, no chasing any little person…just me and my book or thoughts. I had to pay my dues like you are doing and now have a Bank of Memories that bring smiles to my face. This Oak Island Mimi understands more than you know!!

Donna B. I am a beach lover as well. It is my happy place. I again am sitting on the water's edge in my beach chair reading a book. When I close my eyes and hear all of the little ones squealing and playing around me, I long for those days.

Dayton B. Do you not feed the poor little guy?

Kay S. With my niece it was tree bark.

Zena B. When the time comes you will definitely be remembering these mental snapshots. And by the way, this made me remember mine and the tears started flowing.

Teresa G. All babies put everything in their mouths. I think that makes them heatlthy.

Sonja M-C. Believe me, he's not the only child to eat sand and she's not the only to ask questions. That's how they experience and learn.

The Loss of Brown Bear

Maybe yours was a blankie. Maybe it was an old and no-longer-stuffed animal. Maybe a doll that by now has a deformed head, or a dolphin you won from the fair, or a gift someone bought in an airport on their way to see you as a newborn. Mine was Bo-Bo, a small teddy bear. When I was five, I wrapped a hole in his foot with white medical tape and proudly said, "Bo-Bo has a boo-boo."

Lots of kids have one devoted love. A go-to for comfort that's tangible security. They probably sleep with it. If you had one, you know. If you're a parent of a child who has one, you definitely know. If you're asking yourself right now what yours might have been, then you didn't have one. It's a top-of-mind identifiable object.

Parker's is the brown bear you see here. He's aptly named Brown Bear.

Brown Bear watches Parker play and eat. He gets a seat belt in the car and was her date to a wedding. One time we left Brown Bear in Florida and Parker pretty much stayed awake for forty hours straight, waiting for my aunt to kindly overnight him home.

Brown Bear came from former WBTV reporter David Spunt, who gave him as a baby gift when Parker was born. She has maybe fifty-eight or so stuffed animals taking over her room. For whatever reason, Brown Bear is the one that matters.

Actually, he WAS the one that mattered.

I lost him. Parker lost him. Who cares about blame when we had the heart-stopping horror at bedtime upon discovery that he was gone.

Imagine a house being torn apart. Car seats being looked under four times. A stressed-out four-year-old with no way to be soothed, because what she was stressed over was the fact that what soothes her was gone.

It was nearing critical freak-out stage when I suddenly remembered: We'd taken Brown Bear to Walmart earlier in the day!

Oh my God, we'd taken Brown Bear to Walmart earlier in the day.

Oh my God. Walmart.

Twelve hours after rolling away from the worst place in the world you could leave a priceless possession, I was on the phone with a Walmart employee begging her to search their lost and found. Put out an APB. Something. Anything. Help. Help!

She did not seem to understand the desperate severity of the situation. After what felt like eons, she said she'd "go look."

While on hold, I decided I would ask for her personal cell when she got back and text her a picture of Brown Bear. That'd be helpful, right? Not overly invasive on my part?

She returned to the phone.

"We only sell white teddy bears, tan teddy bears, and black teddy bears," she said. "We're out of dark brown."

Forget texting a picture. She thought I was trying to buy a teddy bear at midnight.

I hung up.

Wes threw himself in the car and drove to Walmart. No luck. It was closing time, employees were trying to leave, and there was absolutely no sign of Brown Bear.

Parker only went into a fitful sleep under the empty promises he'd be found when she woke.

I, too, tossed and turned. At 4 a.m., I texted David Spunt's wife Andrea, asking where he'd gotten Brown Bear four years before.

At 7 a.m., I woke up to a teary-eyed Parker tapping my shoulder.

"Mommy," she said sadly. "I didn't have Brown Bear in my bed last night. I think he misses me."

I hugged her so she wouldn't see my tears.

Parker does not believe things unless she KNOWS them herself. She needs explainers and facts and is great with visuals. Which is why we took Parker to Walmart to personally search every aisle. She was on her stomach looking under shelves, calling his name in an adult-like way.

"Brown Bear? Are you here, Brown Bear?"

She was methodical. Hopeful. Serious. And as she searched, I knew. I had known since the word "Walmart" was remembered. I spent every aisle trying to figure out how to explain the fact he was gone for good.

Brown Bear went to college?

Another child wanted to love Brown Bear, too?

He doesn't hate us for leaving him?

In the meantime, I got a return text from Andrea: *David says he got that stuffed animal at Build-a-Bear Workshop. Good luck!*

Google said Build-a-Bear was located at Concord Mills.

But what to tell Parker? I had no idea, but crouched down to her level and opened my mouth. Truth came out.

"Parker, Brown Bear is missing. We shouldn't have left him here. But we did. I know he misses you, but I also know he's okay."

She started crying. Not fake four-year-old drama. Like, true childhood heartache.

She stared at me, huge tears coming down her beautiful cheeks. "But I'm his mama. He needs me."

Those words almost broke me.

"Parker, sweetie, listen. Do you know there are lots of Brown Bears who need a mommy?"

No response. She put her head down. I kept going.

"Would you like to go with me to a store that has lots of Brown Bears? Would you pick out a new Brown Bear who needs love?"

She still wasn't looking at me. I heard a quiet, "But I don't want a new one. I want my old one."

"I know, baby. But Old Brown Bear is gone. Will you at least go with me to see new Brown Bears who need a good mommy like you?"

She nodded while trying to get control of her breathing.

I could see her mind working.

Wes and I got lots of questions on the trip to Concord Mills about how many Brown Bears there are in the world. Are there enough people to love them all? Are there enough mommies? Can she love one Brown Bear and also love another one too? Does Hutch need a Brown Bear? Does Brown Bear have a family?

The talk surrounded stuffed animals, but was 1000% based on real-life attachment and loss.

I tried my best to answer in a straightforward way, but what do I know? What does any parent know? How are you supposed to answer questions hard for any age to understand?

All it did was leave me knowing, without a doubt, age doesn't matter: Love and emotions begin the second we have DNA.

 CS&O

Parker hung outside the Build-a-Bear store, not sure she should enter. She heard an employee explain the process to another child.

"First you pick out a bear…then we stuff him to make him soft… then you pick out a heart and kiss it and we put it inside him…you'll be giving him love! It means he belongs to you!… then we'll sew him up…then you give him a bath…pick out clothes…and name him."

"Brown Bear was naked." Parker entered their conversation. "He's plain. He doesn't want clothes."

I almost cheered. Being stubborn = considering the option.

Here's a picture of how it ended. Spoiler Alert: she was gloriously happy. Even took New Brown Bear on the food court merry-go-round and into the Lego store to show him her favorite things.

New Brown Bear cost $19.26. I would've paid anything to fix her first heartbreak.

CRWD

Three days later I was upstairs.

"Mommy! Mommy! LOOK!"

Parker came barreling into my room.

She was holding two Brown Bears: New Brown Bear and Old Brown Bear.

YOU'VE GOT TO BE KIDDING ME.

"Where did you find him?!"

"He was hiding in my Minnie Mouse dollhouse." She was jumping. Her voice was little-girl shriek. "I forgot, Mommy! I forgot I was playing hide-and-seek with him! I forgot I brought him back from the Walk-Mart Market!"

I didn't know whether to laugh or cry.

"Now I'm mama to TWO Brown Bears! One mama for two Brown

Bears!!" She twirled out of the room, suffocating them with hugs.

My original moral of this story might have been something like...Don't let a child take something irreplaceable to Walmart? Sometimes kids learn adult lessons? Address things directly, and the right words will follow?

Watching your child suffer shatters you as much as it does them?

Maybe now that she's carting around two bears...maybe now the whole point is way more basic:

Don't spend more than $20 bucks on solving your child's drama—there's a good chance the situation might fix itself.

COMMENTS:

Gregory K. Wonderful story, beautifully articulated. Lesson = unconditional love is not always something that we say to others or feel about others. It is what we DO for others.

Millie R. This might be the message I needed today. My husband passed away about three months ago. It was the hardest thing I've ever faced. Today, being Father's Day was emotional. I kept saying, if I could just have you back. I need you. Then in reading this, I saw something in Parker's pain and her loss. But, she realized she could love a new bear as much as she loved old Brown Bear! It helped me realize that just because my heart is broken, I can still love. Thank you, sweet Parker.

Wes C. When I was little I had a blue blanket, "Mott." I guess I was 6 or 7. We were changing planes in Atlanta I think. I left "Mott" on the plane. The airline halted our departure until they got my Mott off the other plane. I remember seeing the guy carrying this old blue blanket like it was a priceless antique.

Adam S. Most of these comments are from ladies. I'll tell y'all my "toy" was a stuffed clown that my great grandmother gave me when I was two years old. Took him everywhere and still have him at the top of my closet now. I am 48 years old and guess will pass him on down. But there's only ONE clown, I have 3 children. I totally know those feelings over the years.

Jennifer E. My son had a Build a Bear named Walt. Walt got his own high chair at restaurants, he went EVERYWHERE with my son until he was about 12. Too old for a bear some would say but my heart was broken the day I saw him put Walt on a shelf. It marked the end of childhood. Let Parker have her New Brown Bear and Old Brown Bear as long as she will hold onto them.

Gaye C. My 25-year-old has a Teddy she got at my baby shower before she was born. Teddy goes everywhere with her to this day. Her flower girl carried her in her wedding and one of my favorite pictures is Teddy sitting on her train of her wedding dress! Priceless! So glad Parker found Brown Bear!

Lyndsey HS. Lacey was honored to take such great care of Teddy that day. Xoxo

JULY

MONTH NINE: Thirty-One and a Half Hours of Freedom

This week was the first day of school for Parker AND Hutch.

The summer program is through a local church we don't even attend. They kindly welcome anyone who'd like to register for half days, three days a week. It lasts three weeks. Add it up and you have a glorious thirty-one and a half hours sans children.

I think they should rename the program: "Sign Up and Save Your Soul!"

SERIOUSLY. SUMMERTIME. HEAT WAVE. LIMITED OUTDOOR ACTIVITIES. TWO KIDS. OUT OF IDEAS. A three-day-a-week drop-off is maybe the greatest suggestion ever. I cherished the time this week as if each minute was a golden drop of water on my parched mouth.

Anyone spending hours and hours with kids in this heat probably gets the point. A break is a dream. This month will go down in memory as "thirty-one and a half hours I get to refill my tank."

After taking this picture on their first day, I packed up Parker, Hutch, their two lunchboxes, her big pink backpack filled only with air and three small crayons, threw two handfuls of diapers in a plastic grocery bag as an afterthought for Hutch, and off we went to "school."

Of the three of us, I was the most excited.

We walked first into Hutch's classroom. I was balancing him on my hip while trying to wipe crusted Cheerios off his face. Another mom was dropping off her little girl. Her baby was strapped into a slick carrier. She was super cute and clean. The mom had notes for the teachers. She was totally composed, going over a baby schedule with the teacher. There was a list and the baby's diaper bag appeared to be packed perfectly.

In comparison…

I plopped Hutch on the floor and said, "He'll take a nap soon. Then he'll eat for a LOOOOOOOnnnnnnggggg time. His food is in this lunchbox." I dropped that throw-away grocery bag of diapers beside him.

…And I was out.

I walked Parker down the hall to her classroom, and when cruising back by Hutch's room near the exit door, I saw the organized, beautiful mom still there, going over instructions.

My competitive instinct took over—I had to look more involved! I had to make sure they knew I was a good mother, too! So I stuck my head back in the room…

All that came out was, "If you have any problems, his older sister

Parker is down the hall."

Brilliant, Molly. Send them to a four-year-old for answers. I hope those teachers were laughing at me later.

I considered skipping to the car. Why? Because I could. I'd dropped the kids off for three and a half hours. I didn't need to go to work yet. I was alone. And if you're alone, you can skip. If you're carrying two lunchboxes, a backpack, a grocery bag of diapers, holding one small hand, and carrying a tank of a toddler on a hip, skipping is not an option.

Sidebar to Parker and/or Hutch: if either of you read this years from now and think I'm a little too overjoyed at dropping you off at "school," please know it's not based on a lack of adoration for you. Look at how ridiculously adorable you are in this photo. Parker—I love that you're a protective big sister. Hutch—I want to eat you up in that little button-down. But these thirty-one hours and thirty minutes this month are my summer treat, and I can't deny the excitement.

You know what I did after I dropped them off? You know what I did that first hour of my precious thirty-one? Nothing. I went home, sat on the couch, looked at the wall, and thought, *I'm doing nothing.*

Couldn't have been happier.

And the best part of having three and a half hours alone, three different days this past week was that when they were over—when I went back to pick them up—I almost skipped across the parking lot to the front door. Not just "because I could."

Because this time, I was ready to see them again.

COMMENTS:

Cynthia S. Molly, as I prepare to send my 18-year-old to college next month, your post made me smile. I remember the 'mom's morning out' days. I felt the same way.

Susan H. Please keep doing updates even when Hutch hits the 12-month mark!! My family dynamic is very similar (8-month-old and 4-year-old) and your stories make me feel better. I sit here wondering if I'm a bad Mom because I struggle daily keeping my little ones busy, happy, and away from electrical cords…and reading your updates I realize the battle is real for all of us. I just keep telling myself that one day I will be the Mom spending half the day on carefully crafted Pinterest projects…but in reality I'll probably never be, and that's okay!

Meg K. Your sweet daughter helped my 2.5 year old at Chick-fil-A playground one day. My daughter gets nervous around the bigger boys and your daughter helped encourage her to climb up to the slide!

 Molly. That warms me, reading something I didn't know.

Leigh Ann D. They grow up and we cherish every memory and even our "alone time" and when we reunite…our heart skips a beat!

Julie C. Skip on, sister!!!

Kenneth W. I want to be the manager for Hutch. We are going to the WWE.

A Daughter

I found myself sitting down to write an unexpected love letter to my four-year-old.

Dear Parker,

I never, ever thought I'd have a little girl. I'm the oldest of four with three brothers. I grew up with them, always had guy friends, never wore makeup until a job required it, and despite my love of high heels, remain most comfortable in jeans and cowboy boots. I just assumed if and when I had kids, I'd have boys.

Of course I'd have boys.

No question, I'd have boys.

I went my entire first pregnancy never asking your sex, knowing in the back of my head I was carrying a son. I knew it had to be a boy.

Because of course I'd have a boy.

No question, I'd have a boy.

When the nurse first said, "It's a girl!" I simply did not believe her. I insisted on checking body parts myself. (Second thing uttered after "It's a girl" was your dad declaring, "Guess now we'll have to pay for a wedding." But I digress.)

I mean, a little girl. A perfect, precious, already loud, teeny-tiny, wrinkled little girl.

We gave you a boy's name.

Pink things immediately started entering our home. Your nursery was blue—because I knew I was having a boy—and the merge of colors began to resemble Pepto Bismol streaks across a Carolina sky.

It was crazy. You were a little girl.

You got older. Started having opinions. Started obsessing over Disney Princesses. Started insisting on only wearing dresses and somewhere along the way you learned how to curtsy. To this day, I love watching you leave a conversation by giving a slight bend of your knees and twirling out of the room as if your exit should be noted.

This is not to say you are prissy. You might be in a dress, but your knees are bloody from falling off your scooter (and getting right back on), there's a stick in your unbrushed hair from rolling down a hill. You're most likely barefoot because, you say, "It's easier to run without shoes."

You're a fearless girly-girl.

The. Best. Kind.

Sometimes I look at you putting together minuscule Lego sets meant for someone twice your age, or see you correctly connect pieces in a 500-piece puzzle, and I want to puff out my chest. I'm already so proud. You're going to grow up and rock the male-dominated engineering field! I just know it!

But the next morning, I watch you lovingly squeeze your toes into small ballet slippers and hear you ask for an "Elsa" braid before dance camp. My dream drifts from science and math equations into graceful, feminine images of tulle and lace and broken-in pointe shoes.

You can be anything you want, my sweet girl.

I like how you like a plan, but also roll with anything. I love how you're tough. Bossy. Resilient. I really love how you're sensitive to other people and don't want to hurt anyone. You know exactly what you want. Usually, you're well-mannered and reliable. Even at four years old. A rule-follower, but already creatively manipulating ways around those rules.

It can be hard to keep up with how your mind works. You never skip a beat. Ever. Your dad and I have to be careful what we tell you because you won't forget.

Most of all, you take pride in being an older sister.

Thank God I didn't have a choice in the matter four years ago.

Love,

Mom

COMMENTS:

Wilsie H. Your love letter to Parker is precious. When you were four we wrote little stories together. You acted them out, like Amelia Bedelia. You had a sign on your door to stay out of your room. You were sweet and so funny. Xoxo I love you, Mom

 Molly. Dear Grammy,
Parker and I love you, too.
Love, Us

Bernadette Z-S. Every age for me was a favorite with Lauren. Each age brought something new in her personality that I loved.

Kelly T. Don't ever stop writing her letters!!!! It's the best thing I did was write to my girls.

Lillian B. Just from what little I have read in the past month or so (new follower), you give her individuality and choices while guiding her in a safe direction to grow. Beautiful love letter. Even when she grows up, in college and as a parent herself, keep the letters coming. I cherish those that my Father wrote to me (one even on a piece of birch bark from a trip to Canada that my parents took).

Sarah R. My girls are an awesome mix of girly and tomboy at the same time too. They can be happy for hours with nothing but a bucket of water and some rocks and dirt and can be found in their tutus helping their daddy work on a car. Not afraid of getting dirty but equally proud to dress in a tiara and "top heels" (this is what they call high heels).

AUGUST

MONTH TEN: Becoming Human

For almost ten months, I have pretty much gotten away with letting Hutch sit in one place. He'll happily stay wherever, quietly, and smile big when I walk by. About a month ago he added "Mama" when I'd pass.

But now we have to actually watch him. If we don't watch, he'll crawl across the kitchen and eat the dog food in the bowl, or hold on to the coffee table and try to grab Parker's kid scissors, or pull himself up on the fireplace landing and slam his head on the brick (thank God for the helmet).

He's becoming a little human. Doors now have to be shut, and gates are ready to be put back up from when Parker needed them last, but his growth is best evidenced at mealtime.

Most ten-month-olds enjoy baby food. Not Hutch. Hutch wants adult food only at every single meal. He had four teeth by four months old, and has nine now. He'll push his bottle away and scream if he sees my plate with STUFF. He'll then take his sweet time chomping away, never getting full. Tonight he ate two hot dogs for dinner. Yesterday, he killed a can of Spaghettios. He also enjoys Fisher's dog food.

Time makes things rosier. So maybe later when memories are fuzzy and it's highlights instead of play-by-play, instead of remembering how I actually feel—like I'm losing hours of life sitting in front of his highchair—I'll fondly recall his jovial nature and know food equals happiness.

෴

These monthly updates started as a way to document life, even when I want to pull out my hair. But now I look forward to writing them. I don't want to skip one, in part because of the comfort you guys bring with your comments and in part because I don't want P and H to read them later and wonder why a month is missing.

I find twisted relief in admitting the flaws. That I miss having time to myself. That Hutch eats sand, dirt, and leaves, and I never hand-sanitize anything that ends up stuck in his mouth. That I've been unsure what to do during a monumental meltdown in the grocery checkout.

But, it also feels good to document the beautiful things. When looking back at Month Ten, I do want to remember how fascinating it is to watch Hutch transition from a round blob to a curious person learning to communicate. He giggles when there's something funny. He gives a battle cry for more food. He rubs his eyes and reaches up for me to grab him to say he's tired.

And every time he puts his head on my shoulder as we walk up the stairs to bed, I forget that I've just spent fifty-eight minutes giving him dinner. At least until breakfast rolls around.

COMMENTS:

Amy L. My daughter is 20 months and only has 9 teeth! And yes, as they get mobile they really get in to things. This is a picture of the most recent Kodak moment. While at first I screamed, my second thought was to grab the camera.

Nancy M. With age, comes memory loss. So you will be able to read about these precious times. My kids are 20 & 15. They have baby books. Not nearly as exciting as a blog.

Larry T. My wife filled up ten journals each for my two daughters as they were growing up. She then gave each one their own book to read, as times were tough and we had very little extra money, my girls have said they never knew we weren't at the top of the money pile because we had LOVE.

Tooney P. Molly for the first time in 12 years I allowed my only child to get so badly sunburnt she blistered, first time ever I trusted her to apply the sunblock, I feel like such a terrible mother!

 Molly. You're just teaching independence.

John L. Molly, I feel like Parker and Hutch are already are talking to one another, I just don't speak their language yet.

Wrong First Day

First day of four-year-old preschool. We prepared last night. Parker picked out her dress and accessories. I packed a lunch. This morning we take "first day photos." Hutch and I get her there a little late…and are confused as to why it's dark and rooms are locked.

Oh. Wait. I'm wrong.

School starts next week.

Happy Monday.

COMMENTS:

Barbara E. I'm laughing. I'm sorry, but I'm laughing really hard. And before you make another mommy oops…next Monday is Labor Day. There is no school, and probably no preschool either.

Dawn C. Well you weren't late then, just very early.

Stacy H. You can definitely NOT deny that she's your child, Molly, she's your mini-me.

Amy H. Molly, don't feel bad. Last year I let my daughter do her hair crazy and wear mismatched socks for Spirit Day. When I got her to school everyone else was dressed in their school uniform; spirit week was the following week!

SEPTEMBER

MONTH ELEVEN: If Hutch Could Talk...

Hey. Mom. Yo! Down here.

I know. You're not used to hearing me say anything other than "MamaMamaMamaMama." But it doesn't mean I don't have thoughts. Here's what's currently on my mind:

1. Keep all music pumping.
2. Copying dance moves is my new favorite thing.
3. I've got rhythm.
4. Have you seen me stand all by myself?
5. Yes! I'm awesome.
6. I'll be walking soon. I plan on being fast and curious.

7. No more bottles. Please. Over them.

8. I want what you're eating.

9. My big sister knows lots of tricks.

10. Like, every morning she comes in my room.

11. She climbs in my crib, turns on the music and tries to sing.

12. She tells me to keep it a "secret" that she woke me up.

13. Guess she doesn't know you hear in the baby monitor, right?

14. She's cool.

15. Do you also know that she carries me when you're not looking?

16. She says that's her job as a big sister.

17. Problem is, I'm more than half her size. It's a rocky trip.

18. For my birthday next month, may I have chocolate cake?

19. Unless there's sand-flavored cake available—yum!

20. I dream about food ALL THE TIME.

21. What's the deal with my helmet?

22. Did I hear you tell someone I get it off in three weeks?

23. Excellent!!

24. I dig being "The Incredible Hutch," but am ready to retire the headgear.

25. You're hugging me even more lately. Please don't stop.

I love you, MamaMamaMamaMama,
Hutch

COMMENTS:

Libby H. My favorite post so far. So cute. So real. What a lovely glimpse into Hutch-world.

Claudette K. In love!! I bet that's EXACTLY what goes on in that sweet little head of his. Go Hutch.

Steven P. Reading your posts makes me wish I would have done the same when my kids were little. Kinda hard carrying those stone tablets though.

Bob G. Yes there are a few men who read Molly's posts and yes, I admit, I am one of them. Your sweet beautiful babies are a lot better news than any other I have heard today.

Kid Mail

It was the most welcome letter to possibly enter our mailbox.

It started three months ago. "Aunt" Kristen Miranda (good friend, honorary title) and I took Parker to the North Carolina Zoo in Asheboro. While there, Parker became obsessed with a mechanical dinosaur exhibit. They were big, believable-looking contraptions with moving necks and an ability to open their mouths and growl.

Parker didn't realize they were fake. Kristen and I never corrected her.

The dinosaur she loved the most was a long-necked fella who ate tall plants, so his teeth were short and rounded. He had a kind look. We snapped a picture as she talked to him. She later asked his name. I made it up.

"Mutt. His name is Mutt."

She talked about Mutt on the way home. The next day. For weeks after. She'd confuse people who had no context when she'd out of the blue tell them, "My friend Mutt misses me. He's at the zoo."

It got to be more and more of a "thing." On various beach trips this summer she talked about Mutt. Asked if dinosaurs liked the ocean. Wondered aloud if Mutt might be too big to build a sand castle. She told extended family about him; they'd then come to me asking, "Who's Mutt?" The explanation would give everyone a cute laugh.

I printed out that picture of her talking to him. She was gleeful over a copy to hold and not just see on my phone. She put it in her room next to her other two most coveted photos—one of her jumping waves, and one with her former babysitter, Andrea, at Andrea's wedding.

About a month after our excursion to the zoo, I started teaching Parker the concept of mail...how to write letters and draw things to send to friends. She loved signing her name, folding up the pictures, sealing envelopes, and putting on stamps.

One morning...

"Mom, I drew this for Mutt. We need to mail it today."

She was very serious. She held up her masterpiece, a picture she'd sketched of Mutt himself. She had the prized photograph from her room in her other hand. She wanted to put that actual photo and the picture she'd drawn together and send it to her dinosaur friend. A true gift from a little girl's heart.

I let her address the envelope with just his name. She paper-clipped the picture to the outside, then ran to the mailbox.

Later, when she wasn't looking, I removed it from the box, put it all in a manila envelope, formally addressed it to the zoo and sent off what I thought might be the world's most darling piece of kid mail.

Since then, she'd occasionally ask if Mutt had gotten her note. I made a dozen mental notes to call the zoo, hoping to get someone on the phone and beg them to send something. I never got around to doing anything.

Fast-forward to this week. A letter in the mail with "PARKER" scratched with black Sharpie on the front.

Inside, a child-like scan of two dinosaurs with a short note.

"Hi, Parker. Thank you for being my friend. I colored this picture 4 U. Love, Mutt."

She was ecstatic. So was I.

"MY FRIEND MUTT WROTE ME BACK!"

In the meantime, I was mentally telepathing silent gigantic thank-you's to the staff in Asheboro. Kinda weird they didn't send a business card or zoo flyer or something…but whatever. Parker was over the moon.

"MUTT WROTE ME BACK!"

Parker ran to her playroom, grabbed her art box and plain paper, and promptly started drawing him a new picture. I could still hear her down the hall.

"MUTT WROTE ME BACK!"

Cℬℰ

Two days ago I was on set during the 5:30 p.m. news when a text came through from my mother-in-law, Parker's Grandma Zizi.

"Did you happen to get Mutt's letter?"

Wait. What?

How did she know Mutt wrote?

It took me an extra heartbeat, but everything suddenly connected. I almost laughed in the middle of some crime alert. (Thankfully, I did not.)

The zoo hadn't replied. That's why there was no business card or contact name.

The letter from Mutt was actually from Wes's mom. She'd remembered her beach conversation with Parker, and Parker later telling her on the phone about writing to her dinosaur friend.

For three months I'd wondered if the zoo would reply, never once thinking outside the box to make up a letter myself. But Zizi had. She'd helped perpetuate her granddaughter's happiness, knowing how special it'd be. She'd made the dream come true.

Innocence creates happiness; letting a child have wide-eyed belief is a gift. Grandparents are brilliant.

COMMENTS:

Terry J. My husband is a mailman. Around Christmas he gets letters to Santa in some mailboxes. He plays Santa and writes back to the child using a red felt tip marker. He has a blast doing it and has even received a few thank you's from parents.

Ashley D. Molly, you make me tear up. It seems you have endless patience and understanding. I have a 4-year-old (as well as a 2-and-a-half-year-old) and I wish I was as compassionate and loving as you appear to be.

 Molly. I do not feel patient. We are harder on our own selves than needed, don't you think? Stop beating yourself up. I bet it's not worth half the bruises you give.

Tracey S. My daughter wrote to Santa every Christmas Eve, she left the note with his cookies. I wrote a reply every year in my left hand. Broke my heart when she finally realized the truth.

Christina T. Love this! My grandfather used to send us letters from the "Florida" tooth fairy and he would have the rabbit in his backyard "call" us on the phone. I think I was 13 or 14 before the innocence and wonder wore off, but always amazed!

Carolyn A. When my daughter was about that age she would get upset when we would check the mail and she would never get anything. Our mailman, who was also a family friend, got wind of this, so he made sure she got something about twice a week, sales paper, junk mail, didn't matter as long as she got something. It's the little things…

Ms. Melanie

This is a tough one to write. I'm not sure where to start.

Yesterday there was a terrible accident in Uptown Charlotte, near 3rd and McDowell. A pickup truck ran into a city bus, hurting sixteen people, killing the driver of the truck. It was breaking news at 5:30 p.m. I was ad-libbing over video from Sky 3 (our helicopter), having no idea at the time that the woman killed was Parker's preschool teacher.

Ms. Melanie could not possibly have loved her classroom of kids more. I am sharing this with you now in order to put a real face on that terrible headline. So many times we hear of accidents and stories, but never know how those people actually impact a community.

I want to be on the record saying that Ms. Melanie Myers impacted a community.

She had been a preschool teacher for a very long time. Just three days ago, Parker got a handwritten thank-you card sent home from Ms. Melanie. She had sent it in return for a picture Parker drew her on the first day of school. Ms. Melanie wrote my four-year-old a thank-you for simply being in the class.

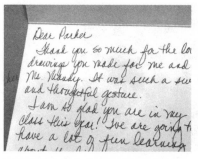

She was that kind of teacher. Warm. Kind. Happy.

Ms. Melanie wasn't married and didn't have kids—the kids she taught were her kids. Her church was her family. Her fellow teachers are grieving in a big way, as are many parents who were blessed enough to have her in their children's lives.

I hope today they can feel hugged knowing Ms. Melanie made a difference. I'm sure she would've been proud to see her fellow teachers this morning. I've never seen such empathetic profession-alism in my life as when dropping Parker off at school. In the face of their own breaking hearts, those teachers were 1000% ready to provide a "normal" day for the kids and provide comfort to any parent who had questions.

Take a moment to think about how precious it all is, and how fast things can change. I didn't know when I saw Ms. Melanie yesterday morning that I wouldn't see her again. Parker didn't know she wouldn't hug her good-bye again. Her amazing coworkers didn't know they'd be walking in today missing her deeply.

I definitely didn't know this morning I'd be helping teach—and everyone connected to that school would be helping teach—Parker and her friends about death.

The little ears listening up at adults explaining why Ms. Melanie is now in Heaven was an image I'll never forget. The teachers were red-eyed and broken, but used soft words to describe how their friend was in a better place. Most kids took it well because, in my assessment, they couldn't process what it meant. I stood on the outside with other parents. The nine kids nodded quietly—they could tell it was a somber situation—but then went off to play as they normally would the first twenty minutes of their day.

Parker, I think, got it. In fact, I know she got it. Afterward she walked over to me. She asked if Miss Melanie was with Pop-Pop.

Pop-Pop is my dad. He died of colon cancer six days after Wes and I got engaged. He wasn't at my wedding and certainly hasn't met Parker and Hutch. We talk about him and show Parker pictures so she knows he's a part of their lives watching from above, but one of my great sadnesses in life is that she'll never actually know him or the depth of his love.

But she does know Pop-Pop is in Heaven. We tell her that all the time. She knows it's a special, coveted place. She also knows she can talk to people who live in Heaven whenever she wants, even in her sleep; she'll just never see them or hear their voice in return.

I told Parker yes, Miss Melanie was now with Pop-Pop.

In her little mind, that meant Miss Melanie was going to be okay, and have an ability to look down from a magical place to check on

Parker and the class whenever she wanted to take a peek. It was all she needed to know. She went off to join her friends who were already playing.

Thank you, Ms. Melanie, for loving our kids so big.

COMMENTS:

Sue G. Thank you for posting this (sad) story and update. We knew Miss Melanie very well too—when we first moved here she was connected to us as a sitter for Katie. She was a trusted babysitter for her with our crazy schedule. Katie still thinks of her today. We are deeply saddened to hear the news and share the fond memories of a lady who so cared for the small children put in her care.

Gray H. Indeed, Ms. Melanie loved our kids so well. Thank you for sharing with others more about what she meant to our community.

Marilyn W. Tonight on the 11 p.m. news, I was astounded at how you held it together and described this woman, then at the end said she was your daughter's Preschool Teacher.

 Molly. Sometimes "news" becomes personal.

Lydia J. Tragic. Thank you for (always) sharing the part of the story that we didn't hear and putting a face on a headline. I'm so sorry for the loss.

Alanna R. I taught that class with Melanie before moving on to teach elementary school a couple years ago. You're right—those kids loved her and she loved them. Her warm and caring spirit will be missed.

Julianne G. I am stunned and heartbroken. Miss Melanie taught my kids years ago and continued to be our go-to babysitter. She was warm and kind, and my kids adore her. This is a huge loss for so many.

Elli H. As Christopher and Nico fight and scream in the next room— Parker's friends in Miss Melanie's class—I struggle with how we are going to tell him this tonight. We didn't send them to school today. This heartfelt message about her will be a good starting point.

Connie R. I had the privilege of singing in our church choir with Melanie. She had a voice of an angel and now she sings among them.

OCTOBER

MONTH TWELVE: A First Birthday

Today Hutch turns one. What is the appropriate way to celebrate?

With Parker's first birthday we did very little. Grandparents in town, a cake at the house, and a pretty day outside. Notably unnotable.

I have friends who blow it out. Clowns, balloons, tons of people, themes, and a pile of gifts in front of a child who won't remember any of it.

For Hutch, I wanted neither. Didn't want to go full tilt, but it has been a long 2015 and I'm grateful to hit his one-year-mark. I wanted to do more than we did for Parker.

I thought and thought, but could not decide. Wes said he was good with "whatever." Finally, we landed on an idea:

Hutch's birthday would become an excuse to have an adult party.

You know that eternal lifelong friend or two you never see? Those few people who are your childhood history? They are woven into the fabric of your life. They are wherever they are managing their lives, and you are moving forward managing yours, but it's an unspoken, known fact you are bonded forever.

Months ago, I called my version of that person and Wes called his. We all marked our calendars to "celebrate Hutch" the second weekend of October.

They flew in Friday, with their kids. My husband's best friend from college, Patrick, and my best friend from the first day of seventh grade, Katrina. Together with their families we had a variety of ages. We caught up, played, found ways to entertain rambunctious children on a rain-filled Saturday in Charlotte, and then our entire hodge-podge of a crew (oldest child was eight, youngest was seven months) went out for a fabulous dinner at an adult Uptown restaurant that didn't even have a kids' menu.

The restaurant had agreed in advance—also agreeing to make chicken fingers and fries—and we got a back room so the kids wouldn't be disruptive. Instead of smothering Hutch with gifts, each child had one at their seat, so each had something to open and an activity to do during dinner.

Then all of us just laughed. Talked. Caught up more. Ate great food. We put Hutch at the head of the table, tied balloons to his high chair, sang to him after dinner, gave him a smash cake to dig his hands into, and called the whole thing a party for him. Which it really wasn't.

But it was perfect.

I highly recommend turning your child's birthday into a reason to celebrate your own past year of getting through newbornhood and balancing life.

If you're doubting me, I'll admit I wondered, too. I mean, who makes a one-year-old's birthday about their own friends? But something else happened this weekend. Something we weren't expecting.

The kids watched us be childlike.

Parker watched me get giddy and silly with Katrina. Katrina's eight-year-old daughter watched her mom laugh for twenty-four hours straight. Plus, the kids formed their own bond. Those two girls were calling each other "cousins" by the end of the weekend. Parker has asked me three times since when we're going to Baltimore to visit them.

There will be plenty of years from here on out where we'll celebrate with a kid affair that a little boy will love. In fact, Hutch, you get to choose what you want next October 11.

But for now, Happy Birthday, big boy. The pictures of your cake are priceless. Thanks for the party.

COMMENTS:

Janet S. What an awesome idea! Now I will copy that to celebrate my terminally ill son's 20th in February! Yes, we will celebrate and I will do everything in my power to make sure he sees #20! Happy Birthday Hutch!

Rebecca W. The cake is fabulous! Where is the helmet? Has he graduated to blond hair?

 Molly. Still wearing helmet. Probably should've mentioned that. Just took it off for the night and for pictures.

Richard G. Thirty years ago my wife and I with our two sons celebrated our closest friend's daughters first birthday almost exactly as you described. The daughter has grown to be a successful member of the media in New York and later back in North Carolina.

Christina T. I don't think you are selfish at all. The kids and adults were included, and you said he can pick when he is old enough to remember.

Wave Off to Work

This is what waved me off to work today.

I burst out laughing, and at the same time my heart melted toward the floorboards. My one-year-old is accustomed to me leaving every afternoon for work…and…he makes me feel like it's okay.

As it happened, as I was laughing, as my heart was forming a puddle, I could only think to A) take a picture and B) park the car and go back inside to give him another hug.

I did both.

Now with Thursday Night Football starting and this photo in

front of my face, I wonder if someday he'll be wearing a different kind of helmet? And instead of waving me good-bye, I'll be a crazy proud mama waving at him from the stands?

Time will tell.

Until then…back to reality. Stuff to do. Newsroom is busy. But I wanted to take a moment to drink in this smile.

COMMENTS:

Lynley B. I call my helmet wearing baby my little linebacker. That picture of Hutch melts my heart.

Laura P. Being a football mom is the best! I have four football players, ranging in age from 8–14. Plus, I'm a team mom, so I have 21 extra boys in my heart too.

Nancy M. OMG, that is priceless. From the mother of a HS football player: DO NOT encourage football. It is so rough. Nothing worse than seeing an ambulance drive up on the field to take a child out on a stretcher. Golf, swimming, tennis. That's where it's at.

Victoria S. You'll have to have someone take it from the other side one day. You waving bye to him. I did it once for my now 18 year old son and put them in frames side by side. Cool perspective.

NOVEMBER

MONTH THIRTEEN: A Helmetless Hutch

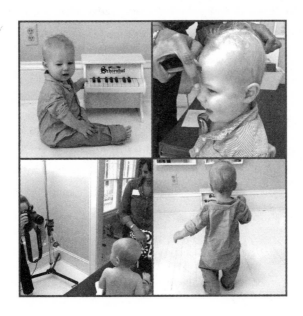

This perfectly shaped head took seven months, three weeks, and five days to mold. Not that anyone has been counting.

This week "The Incredible Hutch" headgear came off for good. He's done!

The ladies at the facility where we had it made measured his head every month. They had a tracking system that showed drastic improvement with technical figures. My measure of success was more visual. When I look at the back of my boy's head, instead of seeing flat and raised on the sides, I now see round and big.

Just like the rest of him.

His day-old hospital pictures showed a perfectly round-shaped noggin. But I laid him down a lot. Too much. Second child syndrome. I was chasing Parker, who needed attention, so Hutch would lie in the swing, or car seat, or on a blanket on the floor. He was quiet and happy, and so was I.

It wasn't until his 4-month checkup that I heard the term *plagiocephaly head*—a fancy name meaning the back of his head was misshapen enough that it was beginning to affect what you'd see when you looked at him from the front. His ears and cheeks and jaw were slowly shifting. They were going to be slanted.

I didn't go into all that detail originally but many of you have asked, so I'm now expanding.

Current measurements show the helmet worked wonders. Even his jaw is back in line.

I hear from other parents with helmet-wearing kids concerned their baby will be mocked.

In almost eight months of my son having an electric-green helmet on his head twenty-three-hours a day, not one person— NOT ONE!—looked at him cross-eyed. I would've called them out if they had.

I had no worries while he wore it. He was protected.

Now that it's off, I'm worried every second because Hutch doesn't know it hurts to bump his head.

Over the past months, he has accidentally slammed himself on a wood floor, brick fireplace, and corner of the table and never felt a thing. That hurts me to even type but I swear to you, he got up each time with no crying or indication he felt pain.

Because of that I'm scared to let him walk. Since we got the helmet off a few days ago, I've turned into an irksome protective parent who doesn't let him out of my sight. He's only three weeks into walking, so he's wobbly anyway…but add in his lack of fear, and I'm hovering like those helicopter moms you see at a park, who walk alongside their child as they explore.

I kinda can't stand me right now.

The good news is, he'll learn. He'll crash a few times, figure out how to be more cautious, and cure me of my paranoia.

The other good news?

His hair. Now I can see it! It's white and long on top. One strand is starting to be curly near the nape of his neck and another is starting to curl behind his left ear. For the past eight months when I leaned down to kiss his head, I ended up kissing painted plastic. Now that he's free, scalp-studying is my new hobby of choice. Yesterday I actually tried to twirl the curl at the bottom as if creating a miniature rattail.

My baby has a new look. These past two days I see my same sweet Hutch, but a whole new child.

I'm glad he had the helmet. It not only reshaped his head, but despite only wearing it for seven months, three weeks, and five days, it cemented him as "The Incredible Hutch" for life.

COMMENTS:

 Molly. Before, halfway through, after (L to R).

Joy Ellen B. Your honesty and 'realness' make you authentic and make the rest of us a little stronger when confronting that voice in our head that tells us we are the only ones who have messy lives, feel fears, and overreact.

Matthew S. My Jaxon is getting ready to be a year old at the end of this month. He is just starting helmet therapy. We have gone a year without being diagnosed even after multiple times of asking his doctors. Finally one agreed and sent us to start the treatment.

Amy M. I love your tough as nails, roly-poly little Incredible Hutch.

Melissa P. So happy for y'all! We met you in the lobby a few weeks ago at the helmet/headband place! We are one week in.

Nancy Cox [former mentor from TV station in Kentucky]. He's perfect in every way. I've never been more proud of you.

Susan W. Has he acted like he misses it, Molly?

 Molly. Yes. He shakes his head and I think he's confused.

NOVEMBER

Mutt Strikes Again

Mutt "sent" more mail. This time, a package.

The freedom to imagine.

Sometimes I wish we could all be four years old.

COMMENTS:

Becca N. I'm so glad we get another Mutt & Parker story. That one stuck with me when I first read it.

Christa H. My friend's mother used to make homemade Raggedy Ann dolls for all her grandchildren. One day one of the poor Anns got left where the family dog had great fun with it. The solution? It was sent to Granny's Doll Hospital, where she was operated on and fixed right up. Grandmas are so special in a child's life. Parker will remember this forever.

Donna W. This makes me smile. I can't wait to do the same.

Kid Art

Today is the day to give thanks. About 45,902 posts in your newsfeed probably remind you of this. Family. Friends. Health. Happiness. A feast.

I'm thankful for Kid Art.

I'm thankful for a little girl who wants to be exactly like me. Who—at the beautiful age of four—does not see my flaws. Who jumps up and down with excitement after a Thanksgiving dinner because instead of cleaning, I ask if she wants to do crafts. Who jumps higher when she hears, "Mommy doesn't have to go to work tonight."

So, with the Carolina Panthers on TV in the background and Hutch soundly napping, Parker and I put an old sheet on the coffee table, get out the rarely touched big bucket filled with small tubes of paint, and dig through the back of our miscellaneous closet (polite name for "where we throw junk").

Miraculously, we find two small canvases I'd bought three years ago simply because they were on sale for $1.99. When something is usually $12 a piece, but marked down to $1.99 for two, a woman feels justified in buying. Whatever it is. We tell ourselves, *Someday I'll need these.*

That someday is tonight.

With two perfectly sized canvases and a place prepared to get messy, Parker and I dig in.

"There are no rules in art," I tell her. "You can make straight lines or circles, you can use just one color or use every color of paint in the bucket. You can draw your favorite animals in the zoo, or write the letters of the alphabet."

She seems to get it. She asks if she can draw Hutch. I say yes. She asks if she can draw her swing-set. I say yes. She asks if she can glue sparkly paper on her "board." I say yes.

I tell her she can do whatever she wants, but we only have the two canvases—one for her and one for me—so she should think about it first.

She does nothing for a minute. I suppose she's thinking.

I pick out the color brown, and start painting the background with wide strokes. Then I pick up blue. I naturally gravitate, always, to oceanside colors and shades of sand.

While I go for the blue, Parker picks up the brown I'd just put down.

I start drawing a tunic. Or, maybe a little girl's dress. I don't know yet. It's unplanned.

Parker starts painting her background brown, using wide strokes.

I paint-sketch an outline and squeeze a blue blob in the middle. I put down the paint bottle to spread the blob around.

She picks up the blue bottle as soon as I leave it on the table.

I now I realize what she's doing.

I decide my blue will be a dress. I get to the very end of it, and while she squeezes out a blue blob... tell her I'll be right back.

I have a small container filled with buttons. All those extra random buttons that come in envelopes on the tags of new clothing? In our house they swim together in one jar. She loves the many colors and sizes you see through the glass when you walk by it high on a shelf. I bring the jar downstairs.

"What are the buttons for, Mommy?" she asks with total excitement.

"You can put anything in art," I tell her. "Remember? No rules. I want to glue buttons on mine."

"I want to glue buttons on mine TOO!"

She wants all black buttons. I grab brown and pearl and small.

Voila! Mommy-daughter art.

The same, yet not the same at all. One's a younger version of the other, with visibly different details in the same shell.

We sign the backs and I date them. The two canvases are staring at us right now from a new, primo location on the living room bookcase.

Tonight, this is what I am grateful for—that for now, at least, in her young eyes, I can do no wrong. Happy Thanksgiving.

COMMENTS:

Kelly B. I am sitting in my chair, full, content, peaceful. Your writing and the glimpse into your personal world is just the star upon my tree.

Emily M. We did canvas art tonight too!

Becky R. "There are no rules in art." I love this comment! I am a retired art teacher and am now able to create art full time. Keep up the great work.

Anissa F-S. I did art with my granddaughter yesterday too. Treasured time.

April C. It's an amazing feeling…One that makes you strive to always be someone that she wants to be like, to make her proud of you.

DECEMBER

MONTH FOURTEEN: Christmas Clutter

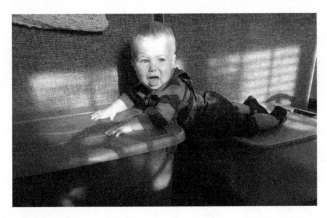

In the midst of dragging out bins of Christmas decorations, Hutch monkeyed up on the boxes and couldn't get down. I took a picture before rescuing him.

A toddler's version of planking. Look at his little dissatisfied face.

These monthly updates (and post or two in between) reflect reality in that moment. Sometimes you get organized musings with clear updates and messages; other times, like tonight, you get clutter. Feels fitting. Matches perfectly with holiday stream of consciousness:

- I hate "Elf on a Shelf."
- I want to be a much better cookie maker.
- White lights + green garland = timeless pretty.

- Idea: Tell your child they can ask Santa for three things.
- Only three.
- I thought it'd teach Parker priorities.
- Limits.
- That she can't have everything all the time.
- Great in concept, only, Parker wants all three to be Lego sets.
- Oh no.
- Wait.
- Am I accidentally teaching her to be laser-focused?
- Obsessed?
- You know, like if you really, really, really like one thing a lot, go over-the-top, dive in deep, never diversify and become completely addicted?
- No. Stop. How very unrealistic.
-
-
-
- Sorry.
-
-
-
- Just had to take a break to sip my Dunkin Donuts coffee and eat a handful of pretzel M&M's while staring at two thousand wine corks I've collected for crafts.
- Next Christmas thought: Do you get gifts for a fourteen-month-old?

- I don't think so.
- All he wants is food anyway.
- Parker made a list for Hutch.
- While hers had three Lego sets…she made his practical:
- "Diapers. Wipes. Book."
- Then she said, "Because he'll share that book with his sister."
- Girls are inherently manipulative.
- Or controlling?
- Or opinionated?
- Or just plain smart.
- Truth is, he would share a book with her.
- He willingly shares everything with her.
- And she willingly shares her entire world with him.

Watching them together is beautiful. Christmastime or not. He's my Nugget and she's my Lovebug.

Two weeks until Santa.

COMMENTS:

Lynn B. I read the coolest post the other day about what to get children for Christmas: One thing they want, one thing they need, something to wear and something to read.

Geri E. Join the club. Elf on a shelf freaks me out.

Amy L. I can't get past the three Lego sets! That is priceless.

Margie R. That photo is a keeper in years to come. He will get a good laugh out of what he did.

Steve M. "Isn't there one string of these lights that works?"

Dianna G. I asked my seven year old grandson what he wanted for Christmas. He held his arms up...looked at me and said "Love and my sisters." He has 3 of them. All I could do was hug him and then he asked for Legos later in the day. Of course I got him those, too.

Eileen F. I despise Elf on a Shelf. Scares me. Yes, you get gifts for a 14-month-old, but don't be surprised if they have more fun with the packaging than the gift.

Tiffany M. I let my three-year-old make a list for her seven-month-old sister too. I think she was just as excited about what her sister should get. There is nothing like watching the two of them together!

Christmas Travel

Look at these two children. So quiet. So sweet. They shared one seat with Brown Bear and Ellyvan, Hutch's version of a precious stuffed animal, the entire hour-long flight to Kentucky last weekend. Most well-behaved four-year-old and fourteen-month-old siblings you've ever seen.

Reminder to a parent: Never get cocky.

This picture shows the trip back.

Early flights are cheaper, which is why we found ourselves in the Louisville airport at 5:55 a.m. Logistics had Wes driving—he'd had to drive to Kentucky because he'd been traveling from work and couldn't get there from Charlotte. I remembered last year's Christmas and our 1800-mile-long car trips with two young kids. If he had to drive, I demanded that the three of us flew. Surely it would be easier.

So at 5:55 a.m., after a few days of family hectic-ness, it's just me, Parker, and Hutch hitting the airport.

Because good planning has us at Louisville International early, I don't mind the frustrations of only one security check line being open, despite two hundred people trying to get through. I remain calm over the extra hold-up when my over-the-counter cough medicine (non-liquid) sets off all kinds of alarms. And the fact that

I have laryngitis and can't talk in more than a whisper doesn't bug me. Instead, it becomes a game for Parker—anything I whisper, she simply repeats out loud on my behalf.

In fact, everyone gets a cute laugh when we finally head out of security and she says, "Thank you, TSA! Mommy says, 'Merry Christmas!'"

We stop at Starbucks and end up at Gate A5, exactly thirty minutes before departure time. About twenty people are waiting as well. There's no sign saying *Charlotte*, or an agent at the desk, but I whisper a question to someone sitting there—Parker asks them out loud—and they confirm they're on the same flight.

Ten minutes later, common sense kicks in, and Parker helps me ask an airline employee if there's a gate change. There is. We're now at Gate A19. The flight is boarding. Parker yells the update to the twenty people around us and they all take off, running.

It is then that Parker has to go potty.

We spend three minutes in a toilet stall. She sings while sitting there, completely unbothered. Hutch tries to crawl out underneath the door. I'm counting seconds. Turns out it's a false alarm. There's no pee. SERIOUSLY??

We book it to A19. It is probably good I can't talk because anything I'd say—like, "WHY WOULDN'T YOU PUT UP A DAMN SIGN ABOUT A GATE CHANGE?!"—wouldn't have been friendly. I am stressed, but we board. We get seated. We even have a few minutes to spare.

It's one of those flights where everyone is quietly settling in, shutting their eyes to relax on a short, early morning trip. It's still dark outside.

Right at this moment, when I'm starting to go back to calm, Hutch decides it's time to play.

He's in my lap and I'm holding his sippy cup of milk and Parker's Starbucks hot chocolate, so I can't do much. Parker starts shoving pieces of her messy double-chocolate muffin into his mouth, creating a flurried brown-looking disaster across our seats. It keeps him from talking.

I love her instinct. I whisper to keep it going.

Soon we're out of muffin, the sippy cup is empty, and we're in line to take off. He lets out a good scream. People look at us. He lets out another, squiggling to get out of my lap. We are the people you hope you're not near. He won't stop shrieking, because I won't let him down.

As this tornado swirls around me, I become acutely aware I'm that mom. Dear God. I'm the mom I hate. The mom I used to roll my eyes over at her lack of controllable children.

But a tornado is a tornado, and you have to react fast, so instantly after that thought I wrestle a Ziploc bag of Goldfish out of the bag under my seat. He generally likes to shake it around, like a rattle, to watch food make noise.

For thirty glorious seconds Hutch is happy, shaking and shaking and shaking that bag.

We are now first in line for takeoff.

All of a sudden…

Yes.

This hurts to type, even 36 hours later...

...three hundred Goldfish go flying.

The Ziploc bag must not have been fully sealed.

I see orange crackers land on people seated around us.

My internal thoughts come out, in a whisper.

Parker hears them.

She yells, "SHIT! Mommy says she wants to die!"

Every head swivels. I can't actually speak, so I raise my hand. I have no idea why. I suppose I'm acknowledging being alive. Parker opens her mouth again.

"Mommy, my teacher says you shouldn't say 'die.' Is 'die' a bad word? Why did you just say a bad word, Mommy?"

At least that's the word she thinks is bad.

I whisper to her I didn't really mean it, as I see people across the aisle pick Goldfish out of their hair. I want to click my heels three times. Transport me anywhere.

As a minuscule silver lining, Hutch is quiet as he shoves fistfuls of Goldfish in his mouth from the now easily-accessible buffet in our laps. And the plane starts to take off, so Parker gets distracted by the speed and pretty sunrise colors in the clouds out her window.

Once the plane is level, I plop Hutch in Parker's lap, take off my seat belt and begin picking up three hundred Goldfish. I don't bother to say "sorry" because I can't talk. I'm also more concerned about the kids. As the second picture shows, neither was thrilled about their new seating arrangement, and I was highly worried about another loud outburst.

Finally, I give up. *Screw it.* I grab the last fish I can and free Hutch to walk up and down the aisle. Probably not the safest decision, but there's no turbulence, and at some point you just do what you have to do. He starts making friends in the way fourteen-month-olds demand attention when they toddle by. He also decides to take a power nap right there in the aisle. I let him.

But here's the thing I notice through this agonizingly long forty-five minutes…

No one is complaining. At least not to me. No one is making me feel like they hate my kids. I guess they probably do (and if I didn't know them and love them endlessly, I would today, too), but no one is letting me know. No one seems to care if Hutch is walking into their space, smiling goofily and yelling some unintelligible word as they try to sleep. Not one of the three passengers who had to step over him napping as they made their way to the lavatory caught my eye or said a word about the obstacle in the aisle.

Maybe the highest standard of humanity happened to be booked on that flight. Maybe there was extra empathy because Hutch had on a Kuechly jersey and it was a plane full of Panthers fans. Maybe the holiday spirit created extra tolerance.

Or maybe they just knew. They'd been there.

Whether planes, trains, or automobiles…traveling is not a treat.

Add in young children and you're on borrowed time, with no idea if that's one hour or eight. On the way to Kentucky, we had a full day of perfection. On the way back, significantly less.

If anyone on that flight from Louisville to Charlotte on Tuesday morning is reading this, I thank you. And I apologize. And no, I don't really want to die.

In fact, I want to let you know the first picture is what I'd frame to show off my kids. The other pictures are reality. Reality may not always be prettier, but (now that I'm a day removed), I know it can be more fun.

COMMENTS:

 Molly: Hutch making friends. Sort of.

Meredith M. We are driving tonight and our three-year-old has a fit because guacamole (avocados are her favorite food) is on top of her burrito bowl. She claims she doesn't like them anymore. Our almost two-year-old is yelling for her pacifier. I start reading your post out loud to my husband and we are laughing out loud. I can hardly contain my composure because I was laughing so hard. I am guilty too of being 'that' mom at one time. But it only took one mortifying experience to have great empathy for everyone in that situation. Thank you for being transparent in your life and making us not feel alone!

Eileen F. When my daughter was about Hutch's age, we were flying from St. Louis to Wilmington through Charlotte. She wasn't feeling well, and insisted on sitting in my lap even though she had her own seat. Just before landing in CLT, she threw up all over me. The flight attendant brought me warm, wet towels to clean up. I had packed a change of clothes for her in our carry-on, but not for me! I smelled lovely. I felt so sorry for the people sitting around me on the next leg of our flight.

Cindy A. News anchors are human too!

Kandi T. Thank you for the chuckle…after all day and week with kids I feel your pain! I'm sure not made to be a stay at home mom… to those who do, KUDOS!!

Melanie B. I laughed until I cried, and then the empathy kicked in.

Kathleen M. Here at 4:58am Christmas Eve, you've helped this stressed out mom/grandma, wondering how in the world I will get everything done, smile and relax.

Tracey K. This brought tears to my eyes. Acknowledgement. Not being afraid to show and share.

Tay H. I just peed when I read about the Goldfish explosion.

JANUARY

MONTH FIFTEEN: To Pull-Up or Pee?

I screwed up. Pretty badly. Mom guilt kicked in.

It came after trying to teach a smart four-and-a-half-year-old to get up in the middle of the night when she had to use the bathroom. I'm sick of buying Pull-Ups, she'll be five in April and it's well past the time for her to be out of a night-time diaper.

Did I ask anyone? No. Did I Google? No. I just knew she'd been potty-trained for years, had no accidents during the day, and Wes and I wanted to get over this overnight diaper thing.

I don't even know why we really cared. Even worse, I begrudgingly admit, I wanted a fast fix.

So…

We sat Parker down and talked with her about nighttime bathroom rules. She looked at us wide-eyed when we said that anytime she feels like going, she just has to get up out of bed, walk across the hall and go. So easy! We'd leave the light on for her. We said many times into her open, absorbing ears, "This is how big girls do it, Parker. This is it."

And if she didn't, we'd take away the privilege of letting her watch cartoons in the morning.

Eek. Aggghhh. That sounds awful to write.

Even worse, it didn't work.

Every morning for a month she woke up in wet sheets, crying that she wasn't "a big girl." Every morning I did her laundry. I was constantly washing sheets, which only made me more determined to get her trained.

A few weeks ago, I tried a new tactic: I'd pull her out of bed when I got home from work between 1 and 2 a.m., carry her across the hall while she gripped my neck in a dead trance, sit her down, and whisper for her to please go. My voice must have soaked into her mind because she'd eventually oblige, fully asleep the whole time.

I'd put her back in bed, and in the morning she'd proudly wake.

It was genius.

Except it wasn't. After three weeks of this dance, I rethought it all. I was teaching her nothing. She didn't even realize she was peeing. Instead of sleepwalking, it was sleep-peeing. All I was doing was falsely bolstering her ego and making more work for myself.

Last week I finally got smart and asked her pediatrician.

"Oh, don't worry about starting overnight potty-training now," her doctor said. "Parker's a motivated little girl. She's moving so fast during the day that when she sleeps, she's zonked out. She has no control. She doesn't even know if she has to pee or not."

What?

"Yes," she continued, "leave the Pull-Ups on."

I told her I'd stopped using them two months ago.

"Were they dry when she woke in the morning?"

No. Never.

"So why did you take them away?

Umm…I just thought by four-and-a-half she should be ready?

"Molly," Parker's doctor stared with a slap-on-the-wrist look, "it's not her fault. Some kids don't get overnight toilet training until they're age six or seven. Sometimes even later."

I told the doctor my enticement: Parker couldn't watch a morning cartoon if she wet the bed.

"You *punished* her?"

Sort of. I mean, Yes.

"You shouldn't do that—you're punishing her for something she has zero ability to control," the pediatrician said. "Consequences should come for other things, not for peeing in a Pull-Up when she's only four and a half."

Painful and deserved lecture. I almost started crying in her office.

CB&O

Why was I obsessed with having my little girl grow up faster? I remember how adamantly I told Parker she didn't need a Pull-Up, when now I know she did, and it hurts me deeply.

The fantastic news is Parker's psyche doesn't appear damaged. She had just as much fun with morning Legos and coloring books as watching *Sofia the First* and *Mickey Mouse Clubhouse*.

And these last few days, she lasted all night with no accidents. I'm not celebrating yet. That could be a coincidence.

So that's this month's memory. As awful as it feels, it's what happened. I thought I knew what was best, but actually knew nothing. Maybe someone else will read this and learn about bed-wetting signs and not issuing consequences for mistakes a child doesn't even know they're making.

The first child really is a guinea pig.

No worries, Hutch. I'm learning as we go.

You get overnight training on your timetable—not mine.

COMMENTS:

Jon H. I raised and potty-trained both my kids. Potty-training is where this Dad earned a few stripes. I let my son streak around the house and when the moment occurred, I picked him up and carried him to the bathroom and acted like Panthers fans act for the first touchdown of the season.

Gena J. We've tried timers, waking up multiple times, stopping drinks hours before bedtime, herbal remedies, etc. We live and we learn.

Yvonne Z. And other mothers will make you feel even worse: "Oh my so and so was fully potty trained at 18 months...Or 2 years..." My daughter was gonna do it when she was ready.

Jennifer E. I was confident my son would start college wearing size 52 pull ups. I felt like a failure. Being a great parent is recognizing you are probably screwing up 50% of the time.

FEBRUARY

Is Social Media Making Us Antisocial?

Saturday morning in San Francisco for the Super Bowl, WBTV producer Corey Schmidt and I were getting breakfast before a marathon workday. Only instead of eating, I was posting a picture on Twitter, Instagram, and Facebook. I was also emailing a quick blog to wbtv.com. Just real fast, you know?

It was justified in my mind. We'd run into an adorable and happy DeAngelo Williams, former Carolina Panthers player. I immediately wanted to share his smile and pink dreads. I wanted to be socially fun. I wanted you guys to know DeAngelo was enjoying life at Super Bowl 50.

In an effort to do so, I was letting my omelet go cold and ignoring the person in front of me.

In an effort to be social, I was being completely antisocial. Corey took this picture and I didn't even know it.

It's twisted. It's rude. I don't like it.

It's not new news that Americans are wholly dependent on their phones. Every time we'd walk into our bustling hotel lobby last week, you could count on two things: HEARING loud chatter and SEEING people look down. If you walked by a group you'd hear words fall out of mouths, but see the person talking not make eye contact with anyone. They were instead looking at their phone. We're no longer talking with people. We're staring at screens while ignoring faces in front of us.

I'm a culprit. This picture says it all.

Corey snapped it to be funny. He says he didn't care that I was on my phone. I believe him. As people who work in the communication field, we're used to watching each other "communicate" with audiences we can't see.

But his picture jogged something in me about the sacrifice of face-to-face talk.

It was definitely more prevalent last week where everyone was coordinating logistics in a crowded big city, but I know it's not just a work-trip thing. People focus on phones everywhere in life. With family. When out with friends. When riding in cars. Even when walking down a hallway. It has become an accepted bad habit. I think we often do it because the person beside us just acted the same way.

I love social media—especially Facebook—and am not going anywhere. I'm here for the long haul. But I love people and actual conversation, too.

Starting now, I'll be more conscious about looking into eyes and valuing both.

COMMENTS:

Elisa N. Just put my phone down, looked over at my guy & grabbed his hand to see him smile back at me—realized I haven't done that in a while. Thanks for putting things into perspective.

Maggie B. In your defense in this situation you were technically working your entire trip—I hung on your every post video and picture and the excitement that was Super Bowl 50! But thank you for this reminder that we need to focus more on people than our devices.

Krista Voda [NASCAR and sports TV host]. THIS is one of my hot button topics. I have multiple bullet points on this very subject in my "things to write about" notepad. Then life takes over and I push the notepad to the side. Thank you for getting there first. I enjoyed your take on it and love the "audiences we don't see" line. Poignant.

 Molly. As much as you do online and on TV, my amazing friend, you SEE everyone. It's why people love you— because you love them. Your little girl is in good hands.

Bob M. Molly, you spoke at my daughter's high school graduation. Your focus of your speech was, "Be social, but not just on social media." That is a phrase we have used several times after you sent them off with the message. But, it fades. It's harder now than it was even then, a few short years ago. Reminders like the one Corey gave you help to reset our awareness level and give a wake-up call.

MONTH SIXTEEN: Freezing Cold and Sunshine-y

I needed a getaway. The kids needed me. Our family needed a break. Welcome to Kure Beach. Two days, just because.

February on the coast. We lasted ten minutes on the sand.

Those ten minutes relaxed me more than any spa treatment. I know my soul. Ever since being a child myself, being near an ocean has been my absolute best medicine.

But at 33 degrees plus whipping wind, Hutch was miserable. His sweet face stayed scrunched.

In a winter coat and four layers of clothes, Parker was trying to build a sandcastle and wade into the ocean in her boots. She is me.

I typed in *Month Sixteen* at the top and doubted it for a minute. I can't believe how old Hutch is getting.

And yet...

...Wes and I want him to get older. Past this sixteen-month-old stage. Wes wants him to age because he's sick of diapers. I wish he could communicate better. We're both ready to go out for dinner and not have Hutch get tired while waiting for food, lose his mind in the high chair, and insist on walking around to other tables while trying to grab at their plates.

Hutch is growing too fast for us, and yet we look ahead.

That's how multiple things felt this month—a simultaneous understanding of opposite extremes. It culminated with the Super Bowl trip. The entire six days I was grateful and thrilled to be in California, away from the daily grind of my kids, but I also couldn't wait to get home and help Parker pick out what she wanted to wear to preschool.

In reverse, they weren't grateful for my time away. They only missed me. Absence made their hearts grow fonder. Parker has said "I love you" multiple times a day this entire week with no prompting, and Hutch gave the most incredible squeeze-my-neck hug when I walked into his room and picked him up out of his crib my first morning home. It was as if he was asking, "Hey there, Mama, where the heck have you been?"

Parker came to visit "Mommy's work" a couple of days ago, and in the course of our newscast, her first baby tooth fell out. She was beside herself with pride, but when she ran over to tell me in a commercial break, she also teared up. She was excited and scared, all at once.

Parker knew the tooth was a sign she was becoming a big girl. She was also frightened in the moment it happened that she was becoming a big girl.

She tried to actually explain that dichotomy on the way home.

It was a four-year-old's weaving description that made no sense. But I knew what she meant. You can simultaneously feel two contrasting things. Proud of your missing tooth, and unsure about why it's gone. Missing your kids while working out of town, and beyond grateful to be three times zones away. Wanting Hutch to mature just a little, while cherishing his beautiful innocence.

Or, as I saw today, freezing cold on a beach washed in sunshine.

Opposites sometimes merge to create truth.

COMMENTS:

Kelly M. I know the feeling! My Yorkie and I came came to Surf Side for the weekend just me and her!!! We lasted about 6 minutes, but got our pic! The beach is my happy place, too.

Laura N. I read your posts like I read a good novel…You have such a gift for expressing the feelings of motherhood. I am sending my triplets off to college in six months, and am actually on a college visit with one of them right now nine hours from home. And suddenly I would give my right arm for a 16-month-old or a four-year-old. Hug them tight and enjoy the ride.

 Molly. Triplets!!?! Wear your halo proudly.

Felicia S. But did Hutch get any sand?

MARCH

MONTH SEVENTEEN: The Things Kids Say

Children are basic, honest, and pinpoint-accurate in how they talk.

Parker never says, "I'm hungry." She says, "My belly would like _____."

Her belly is not yet filled so she decisively asks for _____ to put in it.

Everything she says is 100% literal. When you're four going on five, you say what you mean. You aren't worried where your words will land. You don't sidestep minefields, concerned about other interpretations. You only say what your mind thinks, and no one holds it against you.

At four years old, you say what you ACTUALLY want to say.

I like it. Think how the world would be different if we all just used honest preschool-age directness.

- "If you smell something, I just passed gas."
- "When I grow up I'm going to be a mermaid, because they live at the beach."
- "Mom, I don't like that dress. Makes you look old like Grammy."
- "I'm older than Hutch. That means I'm smarter and bigger. I win."
- "Mom, why do YOU act like YOU make all the rules? You sound like you think you're the boss of everyone and you're not."

In comparison, seventeen-month-olds are raw and rude—and yet direct in their own way.

When Hutch is hungry (pretty much every minute he's awake), he waddles over to the refrigerator and starts pounding on the doors until someone opens them. Then he starts pointing.

While Parker is uber-specific in how to fill her belly, Hutch is like a caveman, grunting acceptance or rejection at items you remove and show. Hutch uses zero words, and yet you have no doubt what he's trying to say.

Both ways are effective, but it's the four-year-old honesty in my head most this month. If you listen closely, the verbal innocence is full of gems.

COMMENTS:

Chris J. Awesome idea to write down the one-liners they say. Wished I had done that. Might start with my twin grand-babies.

Candy P. We went to a Bridal Shower today and my three-year-old granddaughter thought that the bride would get in a shower. I explained we shower her with gifts not water . . .

APRIL

MONTH EIGHTEEN: Turning Five

"Parker likes a good party" is a large understatement.

I used to think that her visualizing exact balloon colors, song playlists, shapes of cakes, outfits to wear, and specific invitations for her dream party was adorable, and her creativity was a sign she'd run a wildly successful event-planning firm in the future. Now I think she could be showing early signs of OCD.

I really don't know if other almost-five-year-olds love throwing a party as much as Parker. Every day—every single day—she rearranges furniture in our living room to "set up for a celebration." She hosts pretend playroom tea sessions with stuffed animals. Her Brown Bears are often on the couch to watch her at a pretend "dance off," that she announces with signs on the front door.

So it was no surprise that Parker was looking forward to her own birthday bash.

She took weeks to map out every detail, even writing her friends' names on cheap brown paper lunch bags she wanted to stuff with bubbles, stickers, and a snack as a take-home favor.

In Parker's mind, nothing was to be spared. This was the Gala of Charlotte.

It began with the cake. Weeks ago Parker asked if we could Google the Frozen sisters to find a specific image she wanted of Anna and Elsa for a simple sheet cake. I liked the idea. Seemed easy enough. Any photo can be screen-printed on a cake at Harris Teeter grocery stores for twenty bucks.

Only, when we found the image and went to the bakery, that's not what happened.

The saleswoman took one look at wide-eyed Parker holding up the picture saved on my phone and said, "Oh, you like 'Frozen'? Have you seen our custom Disney cakes?"

The next thing I knew, Parker was looking through a book, squealing over a two-tiered blue, purple, and icy white concoction of sugar that lit up with a dancing figurine on top.

It was double the price. I'd been duped. The lady smiled—smirked? Selling the child is a great technique. Parents don't stand a chance. Give credit where it's due: this lady knew what she was doing.

And that was just the cake. Parker also woke up every day this week with a loud announcement of how many days until her birthday. On Thursday, her actual birthday, she ran in and said, "Mommy! I'm FIVE! I'll never be FOUR again! And my party is in TWO more days!"

Yesterday afternoon she could barely contain herself. She

was the happiest, most smiley little girl. A walking bundle of self-confidence.

I feel badly for her friends who showed up, ready to be there, but maybe a little surprised to have Parker run to welcome them with a dramatic "HELLO, _____! Come with me and I'll show you around!"—only to be whisked away toward whatever wonder the birthday hostess wanted to show.

The dance studio had old recital costumes, and every child picked one to wear. Parker got to dance in the middle of a circle. Her cake was delicious (though I never did figure out how to make it light up) and she handed out those bags that she'd personally decorated.

The reality of what went down was a sweet ninety-minute get-together at her ballet studio. Boys and girls. The studio provided dress-up clothes and music. We brought pizza and balloons. Nothing too fancy.

But for Parker, the celebration delivered on all her expectations. She fell asleep in the car on the way home, exhausted from a combination of joy and mental energy spent preparing for such an event.

As much as I wonder if all five-year-olds love themselves

this much, my gut tells me that no matter the answer, I'll take her superstar twirling in front of friends...or in front of the Brown Bears stationed on the couch...over a shrug-of-shoulders attitude any day.

Keep dancing, P. I love you.

CRBO

PS: "Month Eighteen" indicates Hutch also just hit a notable half-year milestone. Congrats, buddy. Somehow you got massively overshadowed. Maybe it's the second-child thing, maybe it's because your sister relishes the spotlight, or maybe it's because you're the most content toddler in the world who rolls with everything. No matter why, I officially apologize that this month she takes up a thousand words and you're getting one measly paragraph.

PPS: Take comfort in the fact that we all have another year before she turns six.

COMMENTS:

Michelle K. Don't sweat the cake. They only have one birthday a year. If it makes you feel better, here's my son's custom dinosaurs and trains cake for his 3rd birthday. I won't say what I spent because it doesn't matter. You're a wonderful mama!

Pamela P. Start saving for her wedding.

Peggy W. This coming from the lady that drives from Charlotte to Kure Beach and back in the same day. We all know where Parker gets her energy and excitement. You go, Molly.

Connie C. She is TOTALLY NORMAL! That enthusiasm is not narcissistic but rather joy, wonder, and creativity that should never be stifled!

MAY

Mother's Day

All day I've seen beautiful pictures on Facebook and Instagram of moms with wide smiles. Well-dressed families. Happy kids. Today's weather made for perfect lighting and gorgeous backgrounds. Lots of photos showing grateful, proud women.

Here's mine. This was my Mother's Day brunch.

It was a reservation for ten. My mom, her boyfriend, brother Jay and sister-in-law Amy and their two kids, me and Wes, Parker and Hutch.

My mom was surrounded with family, and the restaurant was busy and lovely. But Parker—who is so often a mature five-year-old—channeled her terrible twos. Total meltdown. Her cousin was sitting in the exact same type of chair, but she wanted his for absolutely no reason. (Reason and practicality do not play a role in toddler-like tantrums.) I made her go sit at a different table to "pout it out."

That was the first half of our Mother's Day meal. My loving daughter in a corner loudly saying, "I don't like you, Mom!"

The second half started when a side of Nutella arrived with Hutch's lunch. Who knew a thick delicious chocolate spread came with kid's pasta? Reread. "Chocolate spread" automatically "came with" the meal. Damn that surely-childless chef and his/her terrible garnish. Hutch had a fistful within seconds. I instantly took the bowl away.

Removing the chocolate elicited shriek-level screaming (you don't mess with Hutch's food), disruptive to every other polite family near our table. I knew we'd be asked to leave if it continued. I caved and gave the bowl back.

Meantime, please remember, Parker was in the corner telling people she hates me.

At some point you've just got to let it go. Find the humor. I ordered a double mimosa.

CR80

Mother's Day is not generally relaxing. Don't get me wrong—a lovely sentiment of a day, but it's not *relaxing*. One family afternoon out or a nice meal made for you is great, but all my friends who are moms of young kids want the same thing. They're just too scared to say it because it doesn't sound nice.

We want time alone.

We don't want to be with the kids at all.

I know how it sounds. I don't really care. It's the truth.

Maybe it's different as the kids get older. Maybe once they're grown and out of your house, you pine for the lunch I had today. I don't know. I just know next Mother's Day I might hire a babysitter.

Or, as Amy said as she fought with her three-year-old to put on a Pull-Up before spending the rest of her Mother's Day traveling six hours in a car with her two kids, "I'm going to pretend next Sunday is Mother's Day. I'm going to reschedule my Mother's Day this year."

She's going to reschedule her Mother's Day!

I don't think she realizes what she just tapped into.

Rather than a calendar telling her when her kids should be on their best behavior and make a day easy, she'll tell the world when she wants her own break.

Let's pick the day. Each one of us individually. Hallmark cards shouldn't dictate our moment—because as evidenced by my brunch today, even the best-made plans can go awry—I think every mom should fit in the special day whenever she actually needs it most.

Amy can take her "Mother's Day" next Sunday. I have a busy next three weeks, so maybe I'll redo my "Mother's Day" in early June.

And then, once we all get our breather from the world of baby wipes and smart-aleck attitudes…once we have serious time alone with no one needing constant attention…we'll be happy to run right back into it.

Promise.

(In the interest of full disclosure, I am now typing this in a comfortable mental state. Hutch got cleaned up. Parker got over her spat and by the end of lunch was in my lap wanting to cuddle.

But I still think one day next month I'm going to find weekend afternoon childcare, call it "My Mother's Day," and experience calm with no kids in sight.)

A huge Happy Mother's Day—whenever you might celebrate yours—to current moms and future mommies-to-be. Here's to the good, bad, and sometimes very, very messy.

It's all beautiful, even when the picture isn't.

COMMENTS:

Lisa S. I have a group of eight friends that when our kids were teenagers, we went to my beach house at Sunset Beach on Mother's Day weekend. Our gift from our husbands and kids. Always came home to dirty kitchens, but it was worth it.

Sarah H. Mad props for capturing motherhood realness. Your candid accounts help us all feel the beauty and the not-so-beauty. They help us feel a sisterhood in mama-hood.

Megan S. My kids are 15, 13 and 8…My Mother's Day gift is a long weekend away with my lifelong girlfriends (the biddies). My husband is going on a golf trip in June for Father's Day. We love our kids, but sometimes you need to take time for yourself, doing what you want!

Lauren V. I hate to admit it but I'm off work tomorrow and I'm dropping the kids off at school and daycare and having a momma day! And nap!!

 Molly. Don't hate to admit it.

Megan T. Beyond true. I usually don't ask for specific gifts because I (tend to) like being surprised. This year, however, has been double the crazy, so I mentioned I would love a massage. Nothing was ever said leading up to this weekend, so I found myself hopeful that a surprise had been planned. No go. I got (lovely) photos and a frame, but definitely no 60-minute heavenly retreat. So I was bummed. And then I felt bad I was bummed. And then it was lunch time and the baby was screaming and I ran out of time to think any more about it. Your post is spot on.

Megan M. If it makes you feel better, my eldest was five when he wrote me his first anti-love note. I'd stuck to my guns on something, and he threw a note at me that said "I hat you." It took every ounce of self-control not to launch into a lesson on the silent "e." He followed it up an hour later with a note that said, "I'm sorry. I love you this much (big heart)" and down in the corner "but I still hat you this much (teeny heart)" Feelings are hard. But they make good stories.

MONTH NINETEEN: Running Late

The calendar was too planned. It was a long week. We had a sick household. Rain made life gray. Whatever the excuse, the day I took this picture I skipped giving baths, let Hutch run around with rat's-nest hair, and kept him in the same pair of pajamas for thirty hours.

Sometimes life is just that way.

Because Hutch was born October 11th, I generally write monthly posts around the 11th of whatever month we're in. Usually. I'm officially behind. That fits with the past week.

Time goes fast. Time goes slowly. I manage it well. It beats me up. It can't be stopped, and constantly ticks to the same unwavering beat.

The clock is a killer. Or can be. And though I don't play everything out in type-A fashion, I do have something preprogrammed in me to always be aware of what has to get done, and by when. I can adapt on the fly but my brain is always firing on all cylinders as it invisibly juggles bullet points.

It's a hard thing to describe. I walk through life with lots of tasks in my head, and each task has multiple steps. I try not to show how I'm thinking about the fact that Steps A and B and C need to be completed before getting to Step D, but D needs to start tomorrow at noon, so we're going to casually do A now and B is set up to be completed during an exact fifty-two-minute dinner break, so therefore C can be completed at midnight, which still gives me twelve hours of wiggle room before D begins.

I try not to let the flowchart in my skull show.

If you are like this too, you don't need me to describe any other detail. You know. We get each other. We're people who absolutely love living in the moment and take everything as it happens WHILE covering up the fact we're also living fifteen-minutes ahead of where we are. Again, not type A. Not necessarily intense. Just...schedulely-aware.

And if you're lost at this point, I wonder what it would be like to be you. I'm jealous in many ways. I love the file cabinets in my brain, but wish they weren't always so full.

(I've been this way since junior high. Drove my mom nuts. She's the exact opposite. I already see pieces of how I work in Parker's personality. It's frightening.)

When you walk through life with a calendar as a mind, you have to learn to have moments…days…maybe even weeks…where you just say, "Forget it all!" You make yourself drop a few balls you juggle. You MAKE YOURSELF. You HAVE TO. A small form of rebellion to keep the calendar from controlling you.

In those moments, you don't care about the flowchart, whether you post your monthly blog eleven days late, or that you let your kids live in pajamas with ratty hair.

Then you enjoy the results. I've looked at this picture multiple times this week. The image is good for my soul. He might be filthy, but he's happy and loved.

Years from now, when I look back on Month Nineteen and see this picture, there's no way I'll remember—or care—that I was running late. Here are the only milestones this month that actually matter:

- Parker's ballet recital.
- Hutch is slow on learning words, but super expressive with facial reactions.
- He purses his lips.
- He laughs big.
- We never doubt what he wants.
- Parker continues to understand him best.
- When I pull out my phone and they know I want to take a picture, Parker slaps on the fakest smile in the history of five-year-olds, and Hutch throws his head back so far you can't see his face, but have a great angle up his nostrils.

- I have a bazillion useless photos in this awful pose.
- Hutch's favorite new food is fried chicken.
- He sits in his high chair and gnaws on chicken thighs.
- Parker is trying to read.
- She has two books—*Madeline* and *Hop on Pop*—memorized.

Until next month (less than three weeks away).

COMMENTS:

Rachelle T. Did you read my brain? Like, 100 percent data capture? Sometimes I feel I need a fake house in the backyard where I can take the kids for quality time, because my real house suffocates me with to-do's and a scrolling calendar.

Dawn R. I'm so feeling this way now. Single mom, my mother in hospital and taking care of 14-month-old. Very frustrated when I can't get things done.

 Molly. Breathe.

Don G. Great-looking young man with a great mentor. His hair you mentioned, looks like his Mom's on the 5:00 p.m. news.

 Molly. Wait—what?

Stephana N. And the World Did Not Come To an End.

JUNE

MONTH TWENTY: Seeing One Week in a Year

We're home. I'm spending tonight going through beach pictures and burst out laughing at this one. Hutch was "King of Kure." At twenty months old, this photo perfectly captures his attitude.

The break was beyond appreciated, despite not being relaxing. It didn't take long to remember how having two little kids at the beach deeply tests the definition of *vacation*.

I am not complaining. The two of them make everything more whole. But Parker is fearless, wholly unafraid of the ocean. She dreams of being a mermaid. Hutch is a loggerhead whose instinct is to rush from a comfortable nest to a wave's edge.

They require constant attention.

To find an hour to myself, I started watching the sunrise at 5:30 a.m. from a beach balcony. In those early mornings I'd sit and look, feel the sun and watch surfers hang on uniquely calm high tides, waiting for waves. My thoughts were silent and warm. Total peace.

As the week went on and my mind sat during this "me" time, I was reminded that though a ruler and a pen scratch will mark a child's growth on a wall, annual trips let you SEE how they age.

Yardsticks show progression. Vacations mark maturity.

2014: Parker wanted to jump waves on the beach where they crashed. She'd wade stomach-high before happily turning around to build a sandcastle. I was pregnant. Hutch didn't even have a name.

2015: Parker was four, bobbing in the ocean up to her shoulders, but mostly begging to go to a postage stamp–sized pool at the place we rented. Hutch was ten months old, took two naps a day, and sat in one place covered in 60 SPF and shoveled sand in his mouth. (My favorite photo ever, Month Eight, last June.)

2016: Parker is five, diving under waves, wiping salt from her eyes and wanting to go, "Farther, Mommy! Farther!" When a wave knocks her she turns to find me, only a few yards behind. Hutch wants to be in the water whether in a diaper, trunks, or fully dressed. He still eats sand, but now uses whatever seashell he finds as a spoon.

In one week of memories, they've grown a year.

Next year, will Parker be on her own boogie board? Will Hutch be talking and finally over the grainy delicacy of the beach?

Writing out that timeline also hints at what's to come. I love Parker's bravado and determination to test limits, but take huge comfort in her still wanting my security when she's tossed down. I sickeningly dread the year she doesn't turn to make sure I'm there.

I love how much they love it.

Sitting here sifting through pictures, I want to jot down things for posterity:

- Fireworks on a beach.
- If you get serious hives (??!?) go to island Urgent Care ASAP.
- Not a fun place for a shot of steroids.
- I'm still sore and embarrassed.
- Beach bedtime is an hour later than normal.
- Early morning walks = sneak your dog on the sand.
- Kure Beach pier still has the best ice cream.
- Hutch is fascinated by the cooler.
- Opens. Laughs. Pulls out food. Closes. Eats. Repeats.
- Parker is more of a hippie than normal at the beach.
- Her hair is in dreadlocks by the end of each day.
- And dear God, she acts older.
- Her personality at five seems so much bigger than four.
- I love hanging with her.
- Turkey sandwiches are almost a requirement for lunch.
- Spray lotion goes fast.
- "Clog-free" still causes zits.
- Best pool is the one that has an ocean breeze.
- 105 degrees is too hot to do anything.
- Hutch's hair is so white it's almost invisible.
- Making friends on vacation is a gift.
- Poolside mojitos.
- Amusement rides make me want claw my eyes out.
- Arcades, too.
- Britt's Donut Shop. What can I say?
- Four visits to get donuts in 9 days.

- (One time even after dinner.)
- Babysitter for one glorious night. Thank you, Maddie.

It's not our last visit for the summer. No way. Only been home a few hours and already miss the sound of waves.

COMMENTS:

Jennifer N. We are also Kure lovers…Love the pier and the ice cream. Britts, there are no words. But I also get hives every summer there. Why? You're the first person that I have heard that from. Curious. Thanks for the moment taking me back to one of the best places I know.

Candyce M. You've cracked me up and made me cry, all at once. Just yesterday, my "baby" finished her sophomore year of high school. The problem is, I'm still trying to get over her being out of Kindergarten.

Becky L. I hope next year Hutch stops eating sand, and Parker goes in the water deeper, but is always looking back for you!

Chris BH. Molly, my Mother passed Tuesday…in the midst of sorrow, Hutch on the beach and Parker as a mermaid brought massive smiles.

JULY

MONTH TWENTY-ONE: Teenager in a Car Seat

She asked for my phone in the car the other day to "look at pictures."

Five minutes later I turned around and almost fell out the passenger side door. Sunglasses on her head (just like me). Legs crossed (just like me). Head buried in a phone (sadly, just like me). The image was striking. It needed no caption.

When did Parker go from five years old to fourteen?

I grabbed Wes's camera and captured the moment before it passed. And then she got bored with silence, uncrossed her legs, took off the sunglasses, and asked some question about a Disney something-or-other. Something that sounded like an almost-kindergartner. I exhaled.

Month Twenty-One. Or as I might as well call it: "I'm Scared."

What happens when Parker stays the way she looks here and

doesn't turn back into my sweet little girl? What happens when she ignores me, talks back, or actually is as cool as she appears?

EVERYONE TELLS YOU TO CHERISH THIS TIME BECAUSE THEY GROW UP TOO FAST. I've said that before, because people say it *all the time*. But God, to live that way is impossible. Each day feels so long. There are moments I mentally beg for an hour alone. I occasionally lock my bedroom door to keep Parker and Hutch out, yell when they're making me late for work, or plop them in front of TV for "just one more" morning cartoon so I can check email.

I admit to all those things.

Even worse, there are times when I catch myself wishing they'd grow up faster so I can have more time to myself.

Then this moment in the car. I see a decade ahead.

No. No. No, no, no, no, no, no, no!

I don't want her to grow up. Seeing her sassy and distant in the backseat makes me hysterical over wasting any minute of our five years so far. Brain-consuming guilt makes me want to launch apologies in her direction: "I'm sorry for locking you out of my room! I'm sorry for yelling when you hid my high heels and Hutch hid the hair dryer! I'll never again choose ten minutes of email over ten minutes with you!"

Seeing her look old makes me think I'm not using my time wisely enough now while she's young.

Every parent has A-ha moments. We all must. I didn't see this one coming. I got slapped with a wildly mature-looking Parker and…I don't know. A ticking clock took over my emotions.

Lucky for me—at least for now—Parker isn't yet a teenager. She is kind, manipulative, funny, and has irritatingly fantastic negotiation skills, but she never looks like anything but a five-year-old girl. (Until this moment.) I take comfort in knowing this photo is a rare peek into the future, but isn't actually the future. She's still just five.

Relief at typing those words. So much so, I will again.

She's still just five.

COMMENTS:

Melissa B. I had a similar moment this evening….when my four-year-old asked if I would visit him when he's in college. The next 14 years flashed before me and I was a sobbing mess.

 Molly. So I'm not nuts. Good.

Lisa S. My most recent A-ha moment was about two months ago. I was at work and holding a patient's baby because he was fussy… When I looked down at that little face I was hit with the reality that my "baby" was going to be graduating from college in a couple of days. Talk about a mess, I cried off and on the rest of the afternoon.

Jennifer J. I am already there with my 13-year-old, and I don't like it! I wish I could go back to when she was Parker's age, and it was just "playing" when she looked like that. Now I find myself wishing time would just slow down.

AUGUST

Cardinal Beach Rules

Our final trip to Kure for the summer. A quick long weekend. My mom is here. So is my oldest of the younger brothers, Jay, with his family. The weather is hot, hot, hot. Sticky sweaty. Crowded beach. We go to Britt's tomorrow. Ice cream later tonight. It's ideal.

Low tide is a dream. Parker and her older cousin went way far out, totally comfortable letting go of my hand. We played "Over or Under," which means right before a wave hits you have to yell how you'll take it. I always tried to jump over (didn't want to lose my sunglasses underneath the water), and they often tried to dive under. Hutch fell asleep on the beach. We all slathered on lotion and got a little too pink. My nose will be peeling by Wednesday.

Parker also got stung by a jellyfish on her right leg. I knew it was bad when she was climbing up my arms screaming "I want Brown Bear!" When she needs my hug AND the coveted stuffed animal, you know she's in as much hurt as a tough five-year-old can be. It was a nasty sting. She made her six-year-old cousin, her best friend and sometimes protector, tell her what he would do to that darn jellyfish if he was able to get his hands on it for her. (He said he'd punch it and throw it in the trash. She told him I probably would've stabbed it with my high heels and Grammy would've stuck it down the garbage disposal.) All things considered, she handled it great. She was even back on the beach an hour later.

I don't want summer to end. It's not over yet—there's still a whole month before school starts. But this will be the last Kure trip for a while, and Kure is my definition of summer. Kure is peace and breeze and who-cares-about-the-phone-or-work-email. Kure is life. Kure is ease. Kure is memories. Kure is my dad. Kure is the past. Kure is the future with my kids.

So when this little trip is over, it feels in some ways like summer is done.

I took every vacation day I was given this year—except Christmas—within an eight-week period in order to spend as much time at the beach as possible. There's still a week coming up this month where we'll travel to see Wes's family. We are excited for that visit, but I can't deny I'll feel a little sentimental catch in my throat when we drive away tomorrow.

There's just something about Kure.

I am starting to feel like a local.

There are things starting to feel like habit, which I don't want forgotten with many months ahead before next year's return.

I don't want to forget my daily morning line to everyone: "If it can't fit in my bag and you're not carrying it to the sand, it's not coming."

I don't want to forget that lotion must be put on inside, and kids' faces need reapplication twice as often as their bodies. Or that if Parker says she's done for the day, I just need to remind her Ariel *The Little Mermaid* princess is somewhere in the ocean. I don't want to forget how to check the tide schedule the day before, or Sunday night's free movie at Carolina Beach Lake. I don't want to forget that the less scheduled the day, the more kids thrive.

I definitely won't forget how baking soda helps jellyfish stings, or how we now feed seagulls from the back of the Southport Ferry, not its second deck like it used to be when I was a child. Rules changed over the years.

I know I'll always remember that morning beach time is the best. How if you wake up, pour coffee in a Yeti, and take the kids in their pajamas, you own the ocean. It's all yours. That's an easy one to never forget. It's not even something you actively recall, it's just part of your soul.

By next year will I forget Frankie's, Uncle Vinnie's, Shuck 'em Shack, or Kure Beach Diner? I don't think I'll ever forget that night our whole big group went out to eat, and it was so busy already that when the ten of us put in our elaborate orders at Gibby's Dock and Dine, it was the final straw for the kitchen staff, and they went on strike. The owners then attempted to grill us free hot dogs.

I don't want to forget that the arcade near Kure Beach Pier is more tolerable than the cheesy Carolina Beach amusement park rides, and my rule on Britt's Donuts—never arrive right at 8:30 a.m. opening. That's when the line is longest. Arrive at 7:45 a.m., when you wait near the front. Or, go at 10 a.m., when the morning rush is done. Or better yet, pack up the car with everyone, *walk into the small old-school donut shop*, sit at the counter, and get served as a seated customer, never having to wait a minute.

I don't think I'll forget that kids go to sleep later than normal at the beach and get up earlier. I'd think it'd be opposite out of exhaustion. But, no.

And that first weekend in June…wow. It's like a ghost town compared to the week after. Guess with Parker in kindergarten this coming year, we can no longer take advantage of that less-crowded time. But it's still something I don't want to forget.

God, Kure. We love you. Thanks for being less than four hours from Charlotte and having such an open invitation. We'll make tomorrow's final day this season really count.

COMMENTS:

Sheila T. Love your rules for the beach. Sorry about the jellyfish sting. Heard they were bad right now. Hope she is doing better. My husband and I went to Britts for the first time several weeks ago. We sat at the counter and ordered.

Geri E. We were in Kure this past week. I fell in love. Told Joe this place is awesome. Next year we will vacation at Kure. We typically stay at Oak Island. It's very quiet and slow. But Kure called out to me as we visited.

Chris E. We love it there too! We were there this weekend too and spent Sunday at the Tiki Bar after visiting Britts.

Chanda A. Britts is tradition but Wake-N-Bake beside Food Lion is amazing. Also, Veggie Wagon is a great spot to grab a beer.

 Molly. Veggie Wagon also has great ice cream sandwiches. Two full cookies—your choice on type—with whatever flavor ice cream smushed in between. Try chocolate chip on one side, peanut butter as the other end, with lemon ice cream in the middle.

MONTH TWENTY-TWO: I'm Raising an Old Man

This week Hutch turned twenty-two months. He has the personality of a grandpa. If he's in HIS chair with a full stomach and drink in hand, he's agreeable. But nothing works if he's hungry. My world stops until he eats.

Here's more proof he should be eight decades older:

- He adores his dog.
- His hair grows in sprouts, mostly on the back of his head.
- He unapologetically burps.
- A lot.
- And the other end. A lot.
- He's mission-oriented.
- Knows where he's headed.
- …But looks aimless. Or cool. I can't decide.
- He waddles.
- Still doesn't talk much, but when he does, not one word is wasted.

- He thinks he's funny.
- Loves me unconditionally, but never says it.
- Gets mad if it's not done his way.
- Wants me nearby, just in case he needs something.
- His name. "Hutch."
- Used to think it was adorably Southern strong.
- Now I think he belongs on a porch with a pipe or a cigar.
- Say it out loud and low. "HUUUUuuuuuuuttttttcchh."
- He likes a routine.
- Knows EXACTLY what book. What toy. What food.
- Things must be step-by-step and in proper order.

Example: He wants a kid "drink yogurt." He leads me to the refrigerator. I open the door. He points to a specific flavor. I hand it to him. He takes the yogurt to the table—still not talking—and puts it down. Then he comes and gets my hand. Leads me to the pantry. I open the doors and he points to straws. He must pick out the color. He takes that straw to the table and lays it next to the yogurt. Then he points to the yogurt indicating he wants me to unpeel the lid. I do. He takes the lid to the trash. He waddles back to the table and puts his arms up so I know to lift him into his booster. Once in the chair, he puts the straw in the yogurt and then—only then—will he drink the whole dang thing, in ten seconds flat. Afterward he lifts his arms back up, meaning "help me to the ground." He's still not talking. He waddles back to the trash to throw away the empty yogurt cup and straw. Because he is never full, we then repeat this process anywhere from two to five times. Always just getting one yogurt out at a time.

He has a similar process for brushing teeth (water goes on first and stays on as he fools with toothpaste), saying good-bye as I go to work (hug and kiss at the back door, then run to the front door to wave), and putting on suntan lotion (he does one leg while I do the other at the same time).

He likes total structure, which makes me want to pull my hair out. Who wants to go through methodical, tedious tasks with a twenty-two-month-old? Though I will say, he's uncannily neat. An odd plus.

Maybe all this structure will go out the window and by his teenage years he'll be a disorganized tornadic disaster living in filth. I'm not worried either way. Because…sure. In moments I want to run away fast. I'm frustrated and tired and can't wait to be in the driveway headed anywhere but our playroom.

But when I back down that drive and look up to see him standing on the front porch, rapidly waving his hand with a goofy smile, I soften. Automatically. If I open the window, I'll hear him chanting his permission to leave.

"Ma-MA! MA-Ma! Buh-Buh, MA-MA!"

I melt. Every time.

So he's a little old-man-ish. That's okay.

He's also a little nugget I get to call mine.

COMMENTS:

Ian T. It's when he tells other kids to get off his lawn that you should worry...

Tracy B. It's a boy thing. The neatness will change around 13 and will remain a mess until...well, my sweet "boy" is 20 so I'm still waiting. When he returns to college I'll clean his room. Enjoy the ride. Those boys are close to momma's heart.

Kim G. Have you been spying on us? This is my little guy to a "T"! His name is Rhett, he just turned two and is a little old man-ish as well. It is a joy and treasure to be a Mama!

John T. Molly, it sounds like he might even be CDO! (That's being so OCD that you even have to have the acronym in alphabetical order.

A Hippie Princess

Parker starts kindergarten this week. For some final summer fun, we went to Asheville for the weekend. Little did I know that my sweet five-year-old would find her inner spirit roaming the streets of Hippie-ville.

I should have seen it coming. Anyone who knows her could've seen it coming. Parker only wants to wear flowy dresses, doesn't like to have her hair brushed, twirls through life, hula hoops like a champ, and is friendly to all.

There was no denying she had found her people and place when a crowd started to form, watching her and her six-year-old girlfriend dance in the downtown fountain. She was barefoot, unbathed, decorated with face paint, and had blue and silver sparkles in her rat's-nest ponytail. She skipped. She practiced ballet. She outstretched her arms in moments as if speaking to the water.

Once they were done dancing, her friend said, "I'm wet and cold." An absolutely normal thing anybody in the universe would think. Instead of agreeing, Parker led her to the middle of the sidewalk and told her they should lie on the brick and let the sunshine hit them.

After they were warm, they led us through an organic festival where they found a bubble machine. Because, of course they'd find a bubble machine in the middle of downtown Asheville. They let the bubbles wrap around their bodies while laughing.

After that, they found kazoos. Because, of course. Of course they'd find kazoos in Asheville. They took their kazoos to a woman sitting on a patchwork quilt, who let them beat drums.

Then the girls were listening intently to an artist who offered to teach them how to weave brightly colored strips of fabric on a loom. I don't know how they found her. She sort of magically appeared.

We ended the afternoon with ice cream.

It sounds like a script. What you'd write if trying to dream up the most quintessentially beautiful, outdoors-y, childlike afternoon possible. I'm not making one bit up. No

embellishment is needed. Our reality was perfect: a gorgeous day with happiness everywhere.

School starts tomorrow for most everyone in our area. Parker's kindergarten is doing a "staggered start," so a small group of kids go Monday, different small group Tuesday and Wednesday and Thursday, then the entire kindergarten goes Friday. It's a smart way to transition into what is bound to feel very new.

So though tomorrow is technically the first day for the district, Parker won't have her first day until midweek.

I have already started laying the groundwork that whether or not she forbids me to try, that morning I will be brushing her hair.

COMMENTS:

Carolyn M. Make sure she gets a good bath tonight. That's where the topless homeless women have taken to bathing.

Suzan R. Your sweet Parker reminds me so much of my Olivia. She is my free spirited Woodstock flower child. She loves flower crowns and still dances up and down the aisle of the grocery store.

Linda H. I raised a hippie and she is kind, sweet and has a real zest for life.

Fran G. My little granddaughter is half Hawaiian and a frilly-dress free spirit. In June, her mother and I took her to Hawaii for a visit with relatives. This picture at her first visit to Waikiki Beach.

First Day of Kindergarten

She was cool as could be. Bus stop and all. I tried not to cry.

SEPTEMBER

MONTH TWENTY-THREE: Absorb. Absorb. Absorb.

Kids are sponges. A secret selfie video Parker made while I was in the shower the other day proves it. I knew she had my phone, but I couldn't see or hear her.

Twelve hours later, standing on set during a commercial break during the 11 p.m. news, I was quietly scrolling through pictures. Sports anchor Delano Little was beside me. He's the one who hit play. We had no idea what was coming.

Watch all thirty-four seconds: *http://tinyurl.com/ParkerSelfie*

If you don't feel like accessing the link (though I recommend you try, simply because her conviction is not able to be transcribed on paper), here is what she said, word-for-word:

"Hello, everyone, we'd love to have you on our WTT Team. It's Molly's Team. Join us, for WTT Team, October first. We'd love to

have you on our WTT Team. It's Molly's Team. She is my...she is the leader, I'm just a kid. But she's the grown-up. And she's my mom. She is strong, powerful, AND in your life. You better hope to come to her station. We'll see you October first!"

I was impressed.

But more proud than impressed, and more stunned than proud.

I was grabbed instantly where she kicked it off with "HELLO, EVERYONE..." as if telling crowds of imaginary people. I re-fell in love every time she said W-T-T as the call letters, instead of WBTV. Delano most appreciated her closing the deal at the end.

It really is something, finding a secret video your child tapes of themselves.

Before making it, five-year-old Parker was (I can only assume) going through my phone pictures and watched a video promo for Komen Charlotte's "Race for the Cure." There are a few on my phone. Parker thinks the "TV ads" I do are funny. Little did I know she also thinks of them as something to copy.

But that's what kids do. They copy. They watch. And often, I'm learning, it's not what you say *but what you do* that makes an impression.

Parker's thirty-four seconds on tape is nothing short of 100% hysterical...and...1,000,000% unnerving. She sees exactly what I do and drinks it up. Bad habits and all, I'm sure. No doubt she thinks flossing is optional, junk food is its own food group, and a cell phone is valued above all.

Which leads me to my next question: If Parker—if all kids—

absorb, can we still TELL them the right way to do things, but continue to ACT differently, hoping they'll listen and not watch? I mean, I have no problem explaining to Parker that she has to floss every morning and night, while doing it less myself. I have no problem telling her that she needs to eat one piece of fruit a day while I grab another handful of pretzel M&M's. I definitely want to teach her the limit of screen time, despite the fact that I—sheesh— break into a cold sweat if I'm away from my phone for an hour.

Yeah. I don't think so.

This secret selfie video is a perfect illustration of "actions speak louder than words." I never taught her how to make a selfie video or shoot a promo. Turns out I didn't need to. She watches how I act and left video proof that she's soaking up every step.

COMMENTS:

Candice B. I. ♥. This. I'm so gonna be there October 1. Wherever there is, because Parker told me to. Awesome stuff right here.

Delethea S. I love WTT!

Brandy E. Tell Parker my three boys and I will follow her orders.

Sandy P. My granddaughter "sells" houses like her mom (real estate agent) on her toy cell phone. Her brother Parker fixes things with anything that resembles a hammer, like his dad (a contractor). They do absorb way more than we realize.

OCTOBER

MONTH TWENTY-FOUR: Happy Birthday Haircut

His sweet white-blond curls were getting stuck inside the back collar of shirts. He'd shake his head after a bath and look like a mop. He had enough for a man bun. It was time.

Or so I thought.

I took Parker and Hutch to Miss Tiffany yesterday for Parker's bi-yearly trim, and Hutch's first haircut. We arrived early morning with Dunkin' Donuts. No one else was in the salon. Miss Tiffany gave us hugs and Parker ran to the shampoo sink. In big-sister fashion, she said she wanted to show Hutch how it was done.

Hutch sat in my lap, across from Tiffany and Parker, with Parker's head leaned back into the sink. Tiffany was asking about her Halloween costume.

Hutch and I listened. He was in front of me. He was very still, calmly eating a Munchkin and watching his sister.

It was a sudden opportunity to simply sit. To breathe. To sip my coffee and not be pulled in another direction by someone needing something. In this unexpected moment of peace, I had a perfect view of his scalp.

It was beautiful. His hair was shiny and soft and swirled in messy perfection. I couldn't stop staring at the back of his head.

In that second, I fell in love with every single translucent strand. The "Incredible Hutch" helmet covered his sweet noggin' the first year of his life, and this second year, it didn't really start growing until the beginning of summer. Now I was going to cut it? *No,* I decided right then. *No. I am not.*

But it's shaggy. My devil's-advocate cynical inner self piped up. *It's too long. It flips in every direction. Aunt Amy had enough to put in a ponytail. He's turning two this week. It's time to start looking like a little boy instead of a baby.*

Yes. Yes! That's right. He IS turning two this week. He IS now going to preschool. Maybe he does need a slightly older style.

As the two sides fought inside me, he turned around. Chocolate donut covered his face. He smiled, open-mouthed. His teeth were filled with chewed-up food.

"Ma-ma."

He laughed. A beautiful baby giggle on a beautiful round baby face. His curls bobbed as his head shook. The noise quieted my devil's advocate. I knew then what to do.

When it was Hutch's turn, he monkeyed up into Miss Tiffany's chair. She put a cape around his neck and started wetting his hair with a spray bottle. Scissors would be next.

"Hey, Tiff?"

"Mm-hmm."

"I just want you to cut one curl."

"What?"

"Just a small piece, please."

"You don't want to cut his hair?"

I felt like she might think I sounded a little odd, but said what I believed. "No. Just one curl. I changed my mind."

She smiled, said nothing, snipped a small section, put the hair on a brown towel and went into a back room. When she was gone, I took a picture of the white blond strands sitting on her table.

She returned with foil and pen. She quickly and quietly wrapped up his blond in the foil and wrote, "Baby Hutch hair" on the outside with the date.

"Here you go," she handed me the small rectangular package.

I smiled gratefully. "I guess you've done this before."

"All the time," she said. "None of us ever want them to grow up."

ᙣᘓᙣᘒ

I continue to find this back-and-forth of raising kids—the "please grow up" versus "no, you're my baby"—a tough dichotomy. I want Hutch to get old enough to be more self-sufficient and easier in life, yet I can't cut infant curls to help make the transition more visible.

Hutch does turn two on Tuesday. This is true. But because I was fully sentimental at yesterday's hair appointment, he'll have baby hair jutting in every direction.

The thought is somewhat comforting.

COMMENTS:

Wendi E. This is my 18-month-old's mop. I just can't cut those curls yet. I haven't cut any of my boys' hair until after their second birthdays.

Elizabeth G. Precious little nephew.

 Molly. I couldn't cut it, Aunt Elizabeth. I just couldn't. Amy really did put it in a ponytail.

Lisa R. I don't think there's a mom alive who hasn't been through the same thing. My daughter, Kelly, had the cutest curls when she was two, but I knew once they were cut off…no more curls! So, her first haircut was when she was three, and I saved a lock, too.

"Mommy Put Fire in My Eye!"

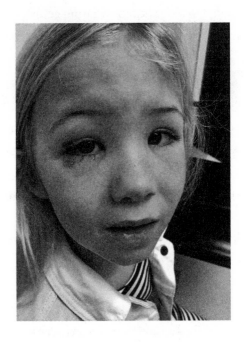

Sunday night we were roasting marshmallows at a bonfire. It was a kids' Halloween party. I was helping Parker and blew large embers off her marshmallow. The wind took those embers and flew them back at her face, right onto her right eye.

She screamed and doubled over, so it took me a solid ten seconds to get the embers off.

I spent the next ten minutes having others help me check her with flashlights. Thank God, not one burning-hot ember went on her eyeball.

Thirty-six hours later, I remain flabbergasted. This whole thing happened in a flash of a second, yet her little eyelid was smart enough to shut fast enough to block her cornea from getting burned.

We put cold compresses and lotion on Sunday evening. She went to bed fine. Blisters popped up by Monday morning. She said it didn't hurt and wanted to go to school.

It was at the bus stop when I heard her holding court, talking about her war wounds, saying, "Mommy put fire in my eye!"

I immediately went home and emailed her kindergarten teacher in case she relayed that storyline in class. I didn't want DSS called. I also called the doctor, who said waiting to come in wouldn't make a difference, and we made an appointment for today. Parker would just be late to school.

So after Hutch's birthday breakfast this morning, he spent his special day in a pediatrician's office overshadowed (once again) by his sister. He didn't seem to care.

The doctor prescribed an antibiotic lotion because skin around the eyes is some of the most fragile we have on our bodies, so keeping it moist will help with keeping bacteria away. She also said if Parker is in direct sunlight, she should wear an eye patch. Parker asked if we could color the eyepatch pink.

The doctor said a few weeks from now it'll be a distant memory. Blisters gone. She'll be fine.

But isn't it crazy how our bodies often protect themselves? How reflexes work? What if—the great "what if"—her body hadn't reacted in such fast fashion?

I can't stop thinking about the natural wonder of us, as people.

PS: Happy Birthday, Hutch. Thanks for constantly going with the flow. I know last year at this time I said you'd get to choose your party this year…I misspoke. Sorry. I have no energy for a toddler party.

COMMENTS:

Diana S. Accidents can happen so quickly. You saying you emailed the teacher reminded me of a saying some of my kids' teachers would tell us in the beginning of the year: "I'll only believe half of what they say happens at home, if you only believe half of what they say happens at school."

Bethany Y. Happy Birthday Hutch! Glad Parker is alright. I once accidentally broke my middle son's finger by closing a bedroom door, not knowing he was on the other side with his hand at the back of the door between the door and doorjamb. So, whenever something comes up about his now crooked finger, it is forever known as "the finger Mama broke."

Lisa R. My oldest daughter was once running with a stick, and I told her to stop or she was going to poke her eye out. Before I could finish my sentence she tripped. Fortunately, the stick caught the inside edge of her eyelid and prevented her from literally poking her eyeball out, but it was scary.

NOVEMBER

Election Day

We voted. And by "we," I mean both Parker and I.

Hers doesn't count, but kudos to whoever decided to implement a K-12 ballot casting table. You write down your school name and check the picture of the person you want for president. Teaching this American gift of democracy at an early age.

Somewhat surprising to me, five-year-old Parker knew the names Donald Trump and Hillary Clinton. She has seen neighborhood signs (for both candidates) and says "older kids" at her school—1st and 2nd graders—talk about the election.

When I told her she was going with me to vote, she went in the playroom. I didn't know it at the time, but she was drawing a picture. It had both candidates' names. She must have heard someone on the morning news refer to "the office of the presidency" because when I asked why a table in the drawing, she said, "a desk for their office."

A kindergartner's interpretation of Election Day.

I don't care who Parker "voted" for. I just love the lesson.

By the way, there was a long line at precinct, filled with happy people and an air of eagerness. No apathy here.

COMMENTS:

Linda P. She looks as if she knows what she's doing.

Amanda M. I wish I had taken my nine-year-old with me this morning because he is so into this political process. But I didn't want to wake him on his day off of school at 6:30 a.m. when I went to vote. Regretting it after I saw the kid voting area set up at my voting place as well.

Marilyn W. This is too cute! Get a nap, you will need it for tonight. It may not be completely over. May just turn out to be a recount from either side . . .

 Molly. Her drawing this morning.

MONTH TWENTY-FIVE: The Dress

She is sad here, but trying to smile "for Santa."

The picture was taken after Parker's most epic nuclear-level meltdown in her five years of existence. We were in a dressing room of my favorite consignment shop, J.T. Posh. The entire boutique could hear Parker lose her mind. Big window into our mother-daughter relationship. Big window into me not having a clue what to do.

I confess this parenting low, because in the written scrapbook of real life it should be remembered, even if unattractive.

Plus, by the end, the joke was on me.

Parker was belligerent because she said she *needed* this dress.

She *needed* a size-2 Kay Unger black mini meant for a woman built like Barbie.

She thought the dress was a long gown for a little girl. She saw it—and I know my daughter and knew what she was thinking—and she thought it was a princess dress meant for child royalty.

As I've said before, anyone who knows Parker knows that she's a sweet, kind, determined, rule-follower. She loves school. But she does have a tendency to glide into a room and curtsy when she leaves. I blame Disney. I don't care about name brands and am not a girly-girl, so it's Walt's fault that my five-year-old feels like designer dresses speak to her.

When Parker asked if she could try it on—I took handfuls of other things to the dressing room, too—it seemed a smart way to keep her occupied.

The dress fell off her instantly. I mean, it was never really on. She stepped into it without undoing any zipper, and held it onto her from the back as she looked in the mirror. The bodice alone was twice her width. She gasped. I thought it was because she realized it resembled an ugly black blanket. I was wrong. She gasped out of a delusional sense of what she saw looking back.

"It's beautiful, Mommy." She was smitten.

It was so long, she was tripping over the bottom.

"It's really pretty, P.," I said. "But it doesn't fit. It's a little big."

"No! It fits me!" She spun in front of the mirror, and the whole thing fell to the floor.

"No, sweetie. It doesn't. It's not a dress for kids. It's for grown-up girls."

"It's only a little big." She pulled it back up and held the back again.

"Parker, I…"

"MOMMY! It fits me!"

She kicked the bottom as she walked out of the dressing room to see the reflection in a bigger hallway mirror. She came back in, still holding the dress up.

"It will fit me even better when I'm six?" A question and a statement.

"No, not six. Maybe when you're sixteen." I remember still smiling at this point. "Take it off please, so we can put it back."

"BUT MOMMY…I WANT THIS DRESS!!!"

Her high-pitched fierceness came out of nowhere. I was stunned.

I bent down to her level and got equally fierce. I told her to get it together. To never talk to her mommy that way. I reiterated we weren't getting the dress. She got louder and louder. At one point she screamed it would fit her when she's six because she'll be "a bigger big girl then." She told me I was mean and was hurting her feelings.

It continued to go sideways. I decided to ignore her. Even though I didn't know exactly what to do, I knew it was a moment where it didn't matter exactly what I did. I could talk calmly, drag her out of the store, yell back, comfort her, spank her, humor her…it wouldn't make a difference. She wasn't listening. She'd fallen off the train.

Crying. Yelling. Everything. For ten minutes.

I continued to pretend to go through things in our back dressing room, keeping her there with me so this explosion didn't detonate the store's center.

At twelve minutes, she looked up. My back was to her and my own head was about to swivel off.

Through sobbing, breath-catching tears, she said, "Mommy?"

I didn't say anything. She sobbed another breath.

"I'm going to ask Santa for this princess dress." She sobbed another one. "It's going to be one of my three things."

My heart sank. I've mentioned how in our world Santa brings three things, and Parker starts making her mental list midsummer. As new toys, engaging commercials, or certain movies pop up, she edits her list. She only replaces things on her list if they're really important. It is (hopefully) teaching her to prioritize in life, and not expect an avalanche of riches. So something has to be majorly significant to claim a top spot from Santa.

Also, her list has been finalized since September.

"Parker…"

"Yes." She stood up. "I am going to ask Santa for this princess dress!"

Oh God. No. I don't want this dress in her closet. I don't want this dress to be something she values. A hot little mini as *the most* valuable item she could own? That's against everything I stand for and what I hope she will someday stand for. Women should be valued for their minds and thoughts and quickness at navigating life. Their hearts and empathy and ability to run the world. Not designer dresses. But I was too late. Telling her she couldn't have it and it was for much bigger girls only made her consider it a prized possession.

"Parker…"

"I'm going to ask for this dress instead of a rocking horse!"

Doomed.

"Rocking horse" had been number-one on her list.

As if to put an exclamation point on me being cornered, she calmly stepped out of the fabric.

"Mommy? Can you take a picture of the dress so I can give it to Santa when I sit in his lap? Then he'll know the exact one."

I hate (read: LOVE) that she's so smart. Now Santa couldn't have an excuse.

I'd been beaten by a five-year-old.

That is why Parker is wearing a sad, fake smile on her red-eyed face. She's hoping to impress the North Pole, despite her attitude the past twelve minutes.

We walked out of the dressing room, and honestly, I still wasn't sure what to do. What would you do? Do you buy it—which let me say was 50% off its already discounted price, then I had another 20% off coupon, then $12 in "buy-back bucks," so the entire dumb dress was only $13?

Or does buying it only encourage ridiculously unacceptable behavior?

We walked out with her believing that it had been left there, and that after she sits in Santa's lap next month—with this picture—elves would make it appear.

But, yes. I spent the thirteen dollars, and this dress was hidden in a bag.

I'm still not sure that it was the right call.

But I do know that for some inexplicable reason, this dress was in her head and she wasn't going to forget about it anytime soon.

There is no lesson in this story. Only horror at how she acted. And how I think I might have caved? Did I? And fear about what loving this dress indicates for the future. I mean, I actually like that she doesn't let me brush her hair, because that wildflower hippie inside her counteracts the glittery-princess part. A little strapless number doesn't mesh with any of it.

Then again, what is my problem? She's only five. Dress-up and dreaming is what it's all about. I need to stop overthinking. Maybe I should just be grateful the number-one thing she wants for Christmas cost thirteen bucks.

I do know this: I can't wait to see what she thinks at sixteen when this dress still hangs in her closet. I bet she won't even like it.

And Parker, let's just say if you read this story ten years from now, I want you to know a few things: I hated your tantrum this past Friday. I also despise the fact that this black mini will be under the tree with your name on it. But I unequivocally adore your sass and style. I love that you're a determined dreamer and can only hope you still live life dead set in your unique desires, constantly working to find loopholes to make things happen the way you want them to go.

This was yet another reminder: I'm in for a ride.

COMMENTS:

J.T. Posh. We all pretended we didn't hear a thing. #MomsWorkHereToo

Claudette Y. You most certainly did not cave. Giving in would have been giving her the dress immediately. The fact that she "wanted" it enough to make it one of the three things from Santa means she figured it out on her own (independent thinker)...calmed herself down enough to share her plan with you (dealt with not getting her way)...asked you to take her picture so Santa would get it exactly right (planning is all in the details)...left the store willing to wait until Christmas to get her perfect princess dress. She did not "beat" you. You gave her twelve LONG minutes to figure it out and she DID. The dress up days will quickly pass but that determination you witnessed on Friday will mature into a life trait.

Margo C. If I could get a Kay Unger for $13, I'd forget the meltdown and hope you both enjoy the dress.

Brittany N. My daughter will be eight and I often find myself arguing with what I'm sure is a smaller version of myself. I get overwhelmed with frustration at times and yet I still admire that fight and determination. I'm hoping I can channel that through the years to create a democratic ruler and not so much a dictator. I too would have bought the dress. I also really like the three gifts idea.

Mary Ellen T. As moms we all have those moments you just can't believe your child is acting that way. She is a very determined five-year-old. If she keeps it on her list, can't wait to see how she reacts when Santa brings it to her. Pictures later please!!

Lora V. This dress, I promise, will one day become a prized treasure of yours. Not hers, but yours.

Nancy L. Thanks for reminding us all that we are one black dress away from making a little girl's dream come true.

Cathy M. Make sure to have the video camera available and ready Christmas morning.

Rose M. This is it! This is the story that forced me to mute the television because my husband's day could only be better if I read this aloud to him.

Janice P. Give her the dress, Molly. Remember you used to wear a tutu and cowboy boots?

 Molly. I remember, Mrs. Phillips. It's spot on with what I still want to wear.

DECEMBER

First Instagram Story

When trying to kick a cold, all you want is sleep. So you give your two-year-old your phone to keep him occupied. For ten minutes he's quiet. You are grateful.

Then texts start coming in. Beep. Beep. Beep. Friends who follow you on Instagram saying they're thrilled you made your first Instagram Story.

Sigh. Hutch still not communicating much with words, but talking to the world with a selfie.

COMMENTS:

Jennifer H. I looked at your Instagram Story several times trying to figure out what you were posting, then read this.

Lori K. This is as funny as when I got my daughter her first 110 camera for Christmas. She went around the house taking pics of all of her pictures on the walls or in photo albums. Never knew it until the film was processed! Kids are wonderful and it's so great to see the world thru their eyes.

Rhonda L. Laughing out loud!

Adele F. You have creative children. Even before they know they're being creative.

Mary R. Last week my husband got a call from my 16-month-old grandson. He talked in baby talk and then hung up. Our daughter had given him the phone so she could have two minutes to wash her face.

MONTH TWENTY-SIX: School Pictures

Hutch's two-year-old preschool photo looks like it's 1978.

I've known his curls were a bit long, but one of his well-intended teachers must have poufed them extra before he sat for the photographer. Surely they did. In everyday life it's a little scraggly and cute, but it's not always THAT…is it?

Regardless, an appointment has been officially made with Miss Tiffany to cut his hair for real after Christmas. I'm on board now. The school picture showed what I couldn't see in day-to-day life.

Then there's his sister. When Parker brought the picture proof sheet home from kindergarten, all I saw was "old." Wow. She's no longer my baby girl. Just like Hutch's, hers proved what I couldn't see in front of me.

I have no idea when the tradition of yearly pictures started in schools, but my Grammy used to pin all her grandchildren, all in those nice little wallet-sizes, on a bulletin board in her front foyer. The first thing any guest would see when walking into her beautiful Victorian Pennsylvania farmhouse was the progression of our year-to-year-to-year lives.

My brother Jay always had an adorable smile. No matter the age or fashion, each year he looked consistently boyish. Fitting. Decades later, he still does.

One year, late eighties, my older cousin, Harty, flipped his shirt collar for his picture. He wanted to look cool. (Think Michael J. Fox's jean jacket in *Back to the Future*.) I remember my aunt was so mad…he must have been ten? Twelve? He never wore it like that, ever, but for that year of life, it's how he was remembered.

The worst by far was my second-grade photo. It reflects a haircut my mom tried to make sound pretty by giving it the name of a famous figure skater: "the Dorothy Hamill." My facial expression conveys what I think about the style. Here is what's important about this stage of life that the school picture doesn't convey: my hair was like Parker's, long and messy. One

day, though, Mom got sick of it and took me to a barber shop—A BARBER SHOP—and had some old man cut my hair into a bowl shape. He'd never cut female hair, and had definitely never cut twelve inches off a seven-year-old girl's hair. It looked horrific. Three decades later, my mom still feels badly. There are very few pictures from those years anywhere in our family history books by design.

Except, of course, my school picture.

A school picture can't be thrown out. It's a marker of time. If you get rid of just one, you miss a year, and just like my Grammy's long row of photos for each grandchild…each and every year needs a slot.

Remembering her bulletin board is comforting to me. I've copied her and have Parker and Hutch now posted in my kitchen on a bulletin board I made out of wine corks. It felt like she was smiling down the day I pinned them up.

Knowing these photos are just the beginning of what will be a long progression is why I have no problem publicly posting Hutch's laughable look. It's just his first one. Maybe next year he'll look a little less disco.

I'll post that one too, as a way to apologize.

COMMENTS:

Kim O. Second grade. What I see when I look at this picture. "Wow look how light my hair was." And the fight I had with my mom for making me wear this itchy scratchy ruffle blouse. And how my grandmother kept it on a similar board for years.

Cristy B. He's making up for the time where his poor pumpkin head and all of its glory was hidden by the helmet. He's like—This Is Me!!! Loud and proud, baby, loud and proud!

Catalina L. So true. Good and bad pics, all are beautiful memories of what was going on at the moment. My children's father got my kids dressed on picture day. I had it all planned and paid for, and I got up late that day. Pictures come home weeks later and I'm sitting there annoyed because they're dressed like clowns. I originally hated them, but realized they were a reflection of a bad but hilarious moment. Good memories.

Shannon J. I chose a blue polo shirt for my son's kindergarten picture. Well, what do you know? His shirt was the same color as the background. Totally blended.

A Strapless Christmas Morning

Santa success! Elves added accessories and princess high heels in Parker's size. The dress needed three clothespins to keep it from slipping down. She was thrilled. Put it on immediately and opened gifts, feeling like royalty.

Santa even left a note. Who would've thought a meltdown in a dressing room weeks ago could create such magic?

COMMENTS:

Mandy M. You can see the spirit of Christmas in her excitement.

Nina T. I must admit a house without children at Christmas is so quiet so I have been looking forward to seeing the excitement at yours.

Beth B. This was such a fun story to follow, Molly. So happy for Parker's magical morning! Merry Christmas!

Kathy H. Been waiting on "little black dress" post. That Santa... he (she?) sure did rock with his (her?) display.

Suzanne M. I also am not a girlie-girl but I do get why Parker had her meltdown. Little girls love playing dress up.

Dawn F. Totally been anticipating the black dress reveal.

Amanda C. I love it! Girl knows what she wants. Just wait until prom time.

Before/After Hutch Hair

I did it. He's no longer my baby. Today Miss Tiffany made him my little boy.

JANUARY

Favorite Photo

Turns out my favorite photo of the whole year was my last day at work before a nine-day Christmas vacation. Parker and Hutch came to the station for a few hours to attend our first-ever holiday party for #MollysKids, amazing kids who live with uphill medical battles. This was snapped outside our studios by friend Chanda Pope.

I love my P & H and could tell you a thousand fascinating nuances about their individual personalities, but now is the first time since December 23 that I've been alone. Wes carted them away for a few hours. I don't know exactly where they all are, and honestly, I don't care. Everyone is safe, happy, and not needing my attention. That's enough for me.

Nine vacation days of twenty-four hours with kids. It gets long.

I appreciate all the Legos, storytelling, bike-riding, closet-cleaning, picking up, eating, eating, eating (and more eating) that we did. I even in some way appreciate the age-appropriate whining, but 216 hours of kids gets me. Mix in family car trips + out-of-town visitors + overall holiday hectic-ness, and after these nine days, I'm ready to go back to work.

Give me a month in the newsroom, and I'll be pining for time at home again. The cycle is real.

One reason I adore this picture is it was taken before the nine days began. I was excited. My expression says what words don't need to describe.

It's a combination of less obvious things that makes it my *favorite* photo from all last year.

One, Parker's wearing her special "winter party dress." Her words. It's a snowy owl print with two velvet bows. She only wears it on special days and chose it that day because she was going to "Mommy's work." (She still calls the station W-T-T, by the way.) She picked this dress to visit my job. In five-year-old language, that tells me all I need to know.

It's a hard thing to explain, but when you're a working parent who constantly wonders if you're slighting someone with your time, knowing your 5-year-old loves seeing your place of employment does something comforting to your own insides.

Another reason this photo will be framed? Hutch's hair. Forever etched in time. If you didn't know him, you might think he was a girl. I love his pre-haircut hair.

And, his hug. Through the photo you can feel his hard hug. He was thrilled to see me walk out the lobby doors.

I love this photo because they didn't know nine days were coming. I did. My expression says how I feel about the upcoming break with them, while they show me they love me that much back.

Back tomorrow with the 5, 6, 7, and 11 p.m. Excited to go at it.

And by the time next Saturday rolls around, I'll be happy to be back with the Legos and bike rides.

COMMENTS:

Betty N. You convey so much more than just your words. This really is raw, honest and beautiful. I didn't have time to read several of your posts over the past two weeks, but I intend to go back to each one. That little black dress is standing out in my mind!

Shannon J. I know the feeling. I've enjoyed my lil' one being home from school, but am ready for him to go back to school.

Bonnie W. As a middle school teacher, I very much look forward to seeing my own kids during school breaks, especially as they have now both reached middle school and I know my time with them will be short. I love the time spent together, the laughs, the jokes, and the togetherness, but I will not be overly sad to return to school.

MONTH TWENTY-SEVEN: Belief in Make-Believe

I spent this weekend as a unicorn. Three paintbrushes plus Parker's imagination. In return, I made her a magical butterfly she named "Sparkle."

A shower has since erased the beautiful yellow horn and pink flowing hair that started on the far side of an eye, crossed my forehead, and waved down my neck. Thirty-six hours later Parker's paint lives on. She's refusing to bathe. ("We can't kill Sparkle, Mom!!")

I love the way she dreams and tells stories and uses expressive behavior. But it's her sense of no boundaries that I love the absolute most.

She sees paint and brushes, but instead of thinking "paper," she automatically thinks "face."

I'm almost disappointed in myself because I would never think "face."

Parker understands restrictions and manners, but rarely sees limitations. Her streaming thoughts often give me new ways to think of things.

Like the black dress. I said no, but she found a detour to make it work. And like I wrote then, "I hate (read: LOVE) the way her mind works."

A free spirit is a beautiful thing to live with, but also feels like a tremendous responsibility to raise. And it makes me fearful to think of her as a teenager. There are too many options. Too many paths she could go down. She's a beautifully obedient rebel now, but what if her "all-in" attitude takes her in a direction of "all-in" that isn't as pragmatic as it should be?

These are the thoughts I have where I try to stop and not get ahead of the moment we're in.

I came home the other day to yet another party being thrown by Brown Bears. When I walked inside, Kidz Bop was playing, and she'd once again rearranged the furniture to create a dance floor. She was twirling in front of "Brown Bear" and "Other Brown Bear," who had prime spots in the middle of the couch to oversee the bash. Didn't matter they can't walk, talk, or plan. Parker wanted them to throw her a party, so she made believe they could.

I've mentioned her parties before in reference to her planning, creative mind. I mention them now because of how easy she makes it. She wanted a party, so she had them throw her one. Just that simple.

Make-believe doesn't have boundaries. Kids don't see the rules the world puts in place. When you're young, you let your imagination go as far as it possibly can, and when it gets to that place, you let it keep going. Parker and I make up stories when I put her to bed (on weekend nights) about dogs that fly and living in princess lands and eating our way through swimming pools of spaghetti. Those elaborate fantasies challenge my mental limitations and are often the best part of the week.

Thinking of ways around the predictability we all know.

Belief in the make-believe.

Using a face as your easel and skin as your canvas.

Beautiful.

CʒᏰↄ

PS: (And now I'm off to convince Parker that even though a bath might wipe off "Sparkle", the butterfly's glittery spirit isn't gone forever. Let's be honest. As awesome as it is to witness a child's imagination, keeping up with it can be a struggle.)

COMMENTS:

 Molly. Sparkle.

Ann C. So why can't she go to school tomorrow with Sparkle? I know, I know. But in the grand scheme of life will it really matter if she and Sparkle go to school one day?

Brian C. My daughter had me made over a few times when she was younger. She's now twelve, and I miss it.

Beverly H. Sparkle is beautiful, just like Parker and her spirit.

Cindy W. Kids can do and go anywhere when they use their lil' minds and full imaginations.

Lynne E. Hope she never loses her inner sparkle.

Hector P. This coming from the woman who has helped cultivate her daughter's mind to believe "Mutt" the dinosaur is real? Where do you think she gets that imagination and belief in the make-believe?

FEBRUARY

Winter at Kure

Cold today? Yes. But also clear and dry. The Super Bowl is tonight, but I don't care about either team. We had absolutely zero else planned for the weekend. Ready, Parker? Ready, Hutch? Ready, Wonderdog Fisher? Yes. It's decided. Wes and I will throw you in car too.

It seems crazy to people when I say that we drop everything and head to Kure Beach for no reason. I used to tap dance all around myself and justify it when people looked at me funny. Now I don't really care. I'm fine shrugging my shoulders and saying, "Yup. Quick beach trip. Just needed it."

It is a need.

Some people do yoga or take occasional spa days. I breathe ocean. A one-day escape carries me through months. Staring at endless waves is meditating and mind-clearing. It's what grounds me. And if I am grounded—or re-grounded, as it might be—then it keeps life's moving pieces grounded as well.

I was cautious in having them bundled up…the day turned out to be 58 degrees. I thought it felt pretty good on the sand, but wasn't sure how they'd react to the chilly weather, being unlike normal beach trips. We'd gone the winter before, but wasn't sure they'd remembered.

There was nothing to worry about. Parker ran down the rickety wooden public-access steps, straight toward the shore with two buckets and a big shovel in hand. We talked about low tide versus high tide, and then I double-checked that I'd brought a bag of crusty bread to feed to the seagulls (though it turned out there were no birds). She dug a huge hole. Chatted away about her castle and its moat. At one point, she ditched her parka and waded into the ocean in her rain boots.

Hutch still tried to eat sand. It's like some bad joke that he still likes sand. But this time he laughed while chewing and added in handfuls of Cheerios.

This February, I saw the beach in their souls. Especially Parker's. It doesn't matter the season or the temperature—they were thrilled to have the ocean within eyesight.

It was a great, great weekend.

I definitely breathed a lot of ocean, and don't feel the need to justify anything.

COMMENTS:

 Molly. Goals.

Bari H. Sometimes I take a day trip. Leave Greensboro around 7 a.m. and leave the beach around 6 p.m. Home by 10 p.m. I understand the need to see and breathe the ocean.

Laura P. Molly, you do what you want. We have literally driven the 4.5 hours to Charleston for the day…just to eat.

Claudette Y. It only sounds "crazy" to people that do not have sand in their blood. The ocean's power to renew the soul doesn't have a thing to do with the season nor the temperature.

Susan C. Isak Dinesen (Karen Blixen) from *Out of Africa* is quoted to have said, "The cure for anything is salt water—sweat, tears or the sea!" My hubby and I have determined it to be true.

MONTH TWENTY-EIGHT: Parenting Is Annoying

I'm posting a super-cute picture of Parker and Hutch to remind me how much I love them. They drove me certifiably nuts this morning.

Being a mom isn't always pretty. Parenting can be annoying. Think I'm terrible for thinking this? Please take the following multiple-choice quiz.

If given the option for a morning routine you would:

A) Negotiate with a kindergartner over how she can't wear a sundress to school because it's cold outside. In response, have her calmly and logically—as if she's in court in front of a jury—explain why every single dress in her closet with any warmth is unacceptable because of "itchy tags," "ugly colors," or, "not a princess dress."

B) Tell your two-year-old he absolutely can't have M&M's for breakfast, and then witness an inexplicable fist-pounding on the refrigerator that would be laughable if it wasn't shattering your brain into a million pieces and making you even more late for a bus stop. In the middle of this tantrum, watch your dog throw up. Then watch the two-year-old put his hands in it.

C) Waste loads of time blocking same two-year-old from taking your keys to your parked car in the driveway, because now he knows how to put those keys in the ignition and will try to drive. With every block of the keys, witness same tantrum described in Option B.

D) Get up when you want, pour coffee when you want, read the paper when you want, check emails when you want, casually text friends, and watch anything that's not a cartoon.

I unapologetically choose D.

I didn't realize how beautiful my mornings were pre-kids until they were gone.

My kids are no different from any other precocious five-year-old and determined two-year-old, frustrated he can't communicate as fast as his little mind thinks. I know that. I get how special they are. I get their quirks and constantly hug and kiss them to say *I love you*.

Because I do. I love them endlessly and unconditionally.

But day-to-day details are killer. Who wants to argue over the color of a dress? Who wants to make breakfast to have it not eaten? Who wants to wait at a school bus stop in the pouring rain only to never have the bus show? Who wants to wrestle a child into a car seat they don't want to sit in, then drive to the first errand of eight with loud wails from the backseat?

Not me. I wouldn't CHOOSE those things.

I DO all of them.

We all do. We do because that's just what we do. We know at some point the clothes battle will subside, breakfast will be appreciated (that feels a long way away), the bus will show, and the car seat struggles will be a distant memory.

But, man-oh-man-oh-man. There are days Parker and I kneel outside her closet, stuck in tedious conversation and I wonder if a secret camera is recording it for blackmail. I never want anyone to hear that back-and-forth bartering.

In the big picture, good overrides the annoying. No competition. Good stuff wins by a million miles. I can take one look at this picture—they love each other so much—and feel my annoyances virtually melt away.

Virtually. Not fully. This morning was a toughie.

I think it's time we admit it. Just say it. Just say it! For all the beauty in mother and fatherhood, *parenting can also be wildly annoying*. Not one soul ever told me I would spend multiple hours in a parked car watching a child turn the windshield wipers on. And off. And on. And off. And on. And off. OH! The hazard button now!? Push it in. And out. And in. And…you get the point.

That age-old phrase, "joys of parenting," holds truth. Many parts are immeasurably joyful. Parker and Hutch are the absolute great joys of my life. But COME ON. We need a new battle cry. "Joys of Parenting" doesn't say it directly. It doesn't hit a soon-to-be-parent with a clear vision of what's headed down their shiny path.

What about, *"Kids: Tiny Versions of Yourself that Pull Patience Apart"*?

Or, *"Parenting: Wouldn't Change Any of it, Except Everything I Want to Change"*?

I'm open to suggestions.

And, next time I go to a baby shower I'll give a "Congratulations" card with my gift, because congrats are certainly in order. But I'm also going to sign it, "Good luck."

COMMENTS:

Whisper B. Sometimes you write exactly what I'm thinking at the exact right moment. It's been a week in my house…so thank you for saying what I was thinking as I sit here drinking my glass of much-needed wine!

Michelle B. Yes! Love my girls and I hate myself sometimes for not being able to appreciate their constant, and I mean CONSTANT, chatter, but sometimes I crave silence—even two minutes of it.

Rebecca R. I vote for *"Kids: Tiny Versions of Yourself that Pull Patience Apart."* Seriously, though.

Denise L. I never envisioned when I dreamed of being a mom that I would one day be having a tear-filled argument about how much toilet paper I used to help her wipe her butt…come on? You're gonna argue with me about the amount of toilet paper I use to help you wipe? You're five!

Shannon T. I tried taking a seven-year-old boy shopping for shoes tonight. Pure torture and no shoes bought.

Angelica H. I think this to myself daily with an almost 9-year-old and a 14-month-old. I'd choose "D" almost every time. Thank you, Molly, for saying what us moms are thinking, just too ashamed to admit.

Phyllis K. Hutch makes me smile. It started with the sand.

Michele B. Nailed it.

Carly H. With a 5-year-old and a 20-month-old, I can relate to ALL of this. I never understood this is what parenting was like.

Mindy A. The "Good Luck" part. Yes.

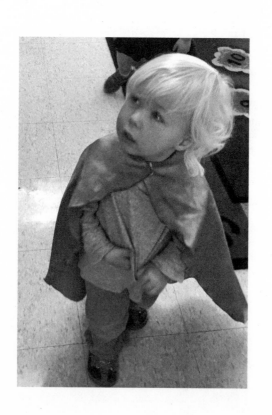

MARCH

A Morning vs. *A Morning*

There are mornings, then there are *mornings*.

After getting Parker to kindergarten forty-five minutes early for Lego class (a real thing), Hutch spilling hot coffee all over me and my white T-shirt (a new one), and Wonderdog Fisher taking a particularly extra-long illegal leash-less stroll around the neighborhood (making me think he was dognapped), I finally get Hutch to preschool. I can't wait to drop him off.

That's when I notice all the parents walking kids in who are wearing green. Oh no. It's "Wear-Green Thursday." I turn around to look at him. Hutch has on gray and khaki. Of course.

As I start to mentally prepare my excuses, I spy a green satiny bit of something sticking out from under Hutch's car seat, where it's been sitting, filthy, stained and disgusting, for who knows how long. Could it be? I reach around and pull out a green super-cape. One Hutch and all his cousins got for Christmas so they could be matching heroes.

Super-Hutch flew into school today.

COMMENTS:

Mary Katherine V. OMG this post just reminded me that it was wear your favorite color of the rainbow today! I forgot. I am almost positive she has on a Trolls shirt which has all of the colors of the rainbow. Bahahahahahaha

Tonia E. My son Gabriel was supposed to wear his Panthers shirt Monday, but I forgot. It happens.

Maddie G. As if he wasn't already the coolest kid in school...

Beth F. I'm like McGyver with what I can do, with what I find under and in between the seats of my minivan. I can feed a family of four for three days on the smashed up goldfish, half eaten suckers and half consumed water bottles alone...

 Molly. Matching cousins. Creative gifts from the always thoughtful Aunt Amy.

MONTH TWENTY-NINE: "It's Broken."

Hutch is playing me on potty-training. He's intentionally controlling the whole process.

Kids are ALWAYS smarter than you think.

This picture was the day we introduced him to the toilet. He didn't want to take off his diaper and sat on it backward like some fool who'd never seen one before. I bought his ignorance hook, line, and sinker. Figured the reverse seated position was a good sign I was trying too early. No worries. We left the bathroom.

The next day—the next day!—his preschool teachers told me how they are so proud of him for telling them when he has to pee.

What?

"Every day when we're outside on the playground, he tells us when he has to go. We bring him in and he uses the bathroom like a big boy."

He says it? Like, actually says the word 'potty'?

"Yes."

He sits in the right direction?

"Of course. He goes, then we take him back out to his class."

I stutter out what great news that is, and thank them for telling me.

Little schemer.

Armed with this new information, the next day about an hour after breakfast, in that always-critical time of corralling them both as we try to get everything moving out the door and to Parker's bus stop dressed halfway-matching, I take Hutch to go potty. It's usually the time he is ready for a diaper change. Not today. Today I march him into the bathroom, pull off his diaper, and sit him on the Elmo training seat.

He looks at me dumbfounded.

"I know you know what's going on here, Hutch," I tell him. "Show Mommy how you pee-pee on the potty."

He stands up and tries to walk away, but gets tripped up by his pants around his ankles.

"No, no, Hutch…it's time to go." I gesture to the potty and sit him back down gently. "Let Mommy see you pee-pee."

He stands up again.

This goes on a few times until he finally understands that I'm not messing around. So he sits. It's all he does. He sits and happily babbles away with words that don't make sense while doing nothing. No pee-pee. Nothing even close. I sit, too, facing him, watching nothing occur. Minutes move. I think of everything else I could be doing. We're now at the absolute last second to leave the house and get to the bus stop on time, so I assume he must not have to go. I put a diaper back on and yell for Parker to grab her backpack…Hutch and I will meet her at the front door.

Ten seconds later she meets us, we walk outside and Hutch looks up at me.

"Pee-pee. Me pee-pee."

I drop down and check. Sure enough, his diaper is wet and full. He laughs. HE LAUGHS. He'd had to pee the whole time, but waited until we left the bathroom to let it go.

Some version of this goes on repeat the next eight mornings. And—I'm not kidding—almost every day his sweet preschool teacher Ms. Jen gives a report about Hutch saying "pee-pee" while on the playground, walking with a teacher inside, and using a toilet.

I start to get more than just frustrated. I start to feel defeated and wholly justified in giving up. The time wasted seems ludicrous. I decide I'm going to stop encouraging him with my high-pitched songs and happy-go-lucky words. Stop sitting annoyed, bored out of my mind, watching the clock, while he does nothing. He'll use the potty at school and not use it at home, and somewhere down the line we'll all get in sync. I don't care. Whatever.

So I stop trying.

A few mornings ago, Hutch is insistently grabbing my phone. He loves to FaceTime his grandparents and entertain them with funny faces. It generally acts as a quick babysitter, so I give in.

"Feeecetime Gigi! Fahcedddime Gigi! Mommy phone!"

Gigi is my stepmom. I put Hutch on my lap and we get her on

the phone. She laughs at him for sixty seconds before turning her attention to me to ask about Easter vacation plans.

Out of nowhere he says, "Pee-pee."

He wriggles off my lap and heads to the bathroom. While still on Facetime, I follow. I'm not paying full attention because Gigi is asking in-depth questions about schedules and flights. I notice he's taking off his pants and now untaping his own diaper, but I don't register the actions. Seeing, but not processing. He sits on Elmo.

And suddenly I put it all together.

"Gigi—hold on. I think he's about to go to the bathroom." I turn the phone around so she can watch. (Because this is what crazy moms instinctively do, and what beloved grandmothers want to see.)

"Come on Hutch," I say. "Show me how you pee-pee in the potty!"

Nothing. I try again. Still nothing. I try again. It's as if he doesn't hear me.

"Hey Hutch-boy," Gigi chimes in. "Can you show Gigi how you go?"

He looks down, and I swear on my life, starts going.

"OH, HUTCH! You're peeing for Gigi!" My stepmom is giggling like a schoolgirl from her home in Florida. He looks up—to the phone, not me—beaming ear-to-ear.

"Hutch, I'm SO PROUD OF YOU!!" Gigi squeals. "You pee-peed in the potty for Gigi!"

Yes. He had pee-peed in the potty. Once again, for someone else.

I wasn't mad, though. It was exciting to personally see him connect the dots and show that he understood the process. One more step to becoming a big boy.

"Are you done?" Gigi asks through the phone.

He is clearly done. There is no more. But instead of replying "yes" he looks down at himself and says clear as day, "It's broken. All done. It's broken."

We both lost our minds laughing.

Later she told me, "You better write that one down."

A week later, Hutch still won't use the potty for me. It's obviously a game where he likes to impress others and doesn't care about impressing his mother. That's okay. It's a great reminder if you try and push and try and push, you lose. Even at twenty-nine months old, they have a mind of their own.

COMMENTS:

Vicky V. OMG Molly I laughed out loud several times. I could just see you sitting there waiting, because you had a dozen other things to do. Of course you know he will get it and he will try to "play" you.

Amy R. My son is just a few weeks younger than Hutch. He can take off his diaper and loves to pee in random spots in the house. Never the toilet.

Sandra J. Act as if you're not paying any attention to him. He will do it.

Millicent H. Hutch has your number.

APRIL

It Takes a Village

I am at work. In comes this email. One of Hutch's amazingly kind teachers knows me well enough to somehow know I already had this mixed up in my mind, and was planning to send Hutch to school Monday and keep Parker home.

Do you think it was the day Parker arrived to her first day of four-year-old class a week early? Or the day Hutch came to "wear green day" in gray and khaki? Or, maybe, it was the time I forgot picture day and Parker looked homeless?

This is classic and perfect and I love this email and THANK YOU to the wonderful teacher who knows exactly who she is. It takes a village.

COMMENTS:

Susan R. I love the translations in parentheses…just in case you didn't understand the meaning the first time.

Megan M. "I know in the past you have struggled with this." I'm dying.

Jennifer W. I struggle keeping these things straight and my kiddos are still at the same preschool…where I'm also a teacher.

Elisa DM. That is a classic! Miss X needs an extra special teacher's gift this year.

MONTH THIRTY: Getting Her Ears Pinched

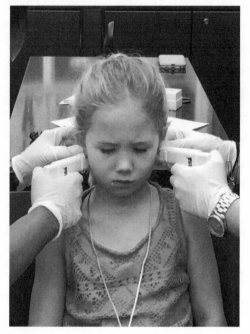

A little less than a year ago I was brushing Parker's hair. We were both looking in the mirror.

"Mommy?"

Yes.

"For my next birthday, I want to get my ears pinched."

It took me a minute. To my credit, I didn't laugh out loud. Instead I asked why.

"Because big girls have their ears pinched. And you have your ears pinched. And princesses have their ears pinched, too."

I told her we could talk about it closer to her birthday, knowing that was eleven months off. It was the best I could do in the moment. I didn't know if I was ready for her to have pierced ears and didn't want to make that decision rapidly, so I deflected. She accepted my answer and that was the end of it.

Until last month.

"Mommy?"

Yes.

"Remember you said we could talk about getting my ears pinched when I turn six?"

In dealing with Parker you only need to remember: She Never Forgets Anything. Her mind is a trap. Not a sand trap where you can maybe get out of it if you take a lucky swing. No. Her mind is a Venus Fly Trap. The kind of trap where you don't stand a chance. She chews on thoughts until she's satiated. Parker blurts out weekly memories from when she was two years old and in diapers, barely able to use sentences. Her mind remembers routes in Charlotte and she can give directions to places she has only been a few times. She can describe minute details of every dress she has owned over the past three years.

So this comment wasn't a surprise, as much as it caught me off guard.

I didn't know what I thought. Was it okay for my six-year-old to get her ears pierced for her birthday gift? Or is that too young? I asked Wes. He didn't have a strong opinion either way. I told him I had gotten mine pierced for my seventh birthday at a Piercing Pagoda kiosk in a mall in Lancaster, Pennsylvania, and six isn't that far from seven. We decided to surprise her with the gift.

This past Friday morning, she woke up to find three gift bags at the breakfast table. (Hutch couldn't've cared less, fully distracted by Dunkin' Donuts chocolate muffins.) But Parker saw the presents and started jumping up and down. She knew they were all for her.

She opened the first one: a new bathing suit with starfish. The second had Kidz Bop CD's. The third bag was confusing: an empty jewelry box.

I pulled out the laptop from behind the table. I already had it loaded with the Piercing Pagoda homepage (the same jewelry chain is still around!), with dozens of photos showing small earrings.

I told her she got to pick out one pair and the next day we had an appointment at the mall to get her ears pierced.

SHE SQUEALED. Grabbed the computer and went to the couch to immediately scroll around and look at her options.

CR80

If you have a daughter and haven't yet gotten her ears pierced, take my advice and don't plan to take her to the ear-piercing appointment right after her birthday party. Poor Parker was so tired she had me carry her into the mall. The combination of excitement and exhaustion was almost too much for a newly-turned-six-year-old to bear.

Almost too much. Five steps into Carolina Place Mall, her second wind arrived. She asked me to put her down.

She walked ahead of me to the map directory. Made me show where we were going compared to where we were. Then she led the way. When we arrived, she walked up to the glass counters and looked at the "starter sets." Took exactly one second to point to little gold dolphins with a cubic zirconia speck of a sparkle in the tail she had seen online the day before.

Manager Miss Lynn introduced herself. Parker wouldn't talk. Every question Lynn asked, Parker responded with nods or head shakes. Parker was looking at her intensely, but never said one syllable.

Lynn had no idea Parker is usually a chatterbox, so she didn't think anything of it. I assumed Parker's unusual silence was a sign she was nervous.

Lynn went over all the rules. "Clean them twice a day, morning and night...Don't take them out for eight weeks...Come back for a free check so we can make sure your ears are healing well... You must have an earring in the holes at all times for the first six months..."

Lynn had a calm voice and open smile and went on and on. Parker looked at her steadily, nodding, never uttering a word.

Then Lynn told Parker to come behind the counter and hop in the chair.

Truth be told, I thought she might hesitate.

She didn't. She walked right into that kiosk and climbed up. She chewed on the ends of her ponytail while watching Lynn move around. Her stoic face never caught my eye once.

Then Lynn asked me if I wanted it done "double."

What?

"If another employee and I both use a piercing tool at the same time, one on each of her ears, it'll only hurt once. It looks like a bigger deal to you as a parent, but it's more efficient."

Great.

It took what felt like forever. Marking the earlobes. Checking symmetry. Sanitizing everything. Then suddenly two women, two piercing guns, one Parker, and BAM! They shot those needles right through her lobes.

My girl didn't flinch once and made no noise. She kept her eyes closed even after it was over, until Lynn happily said, "You did it! Your ears are pierced!"

Parker took the mirror Lynn handed her and moved her head side to side. She did this a few times. She still didn't say anything. I think even Lynn was surprised at the lack of reaction.

"Do you like them?"

Parker nodded up at Lynn in approval.

She wiggled off the chair and came to me. I crouched down. I could tell by now she didn't want high-pitched voices or me acting a fool with dramatic excitement, so I simply hugged her tight and whispered, "They look beautiful, Parker. I am proud of my big girl."

She replied quietly by asking if we could take a picture together.

And that was it. There was never a major moment. She didn't inspect her ears the whole way home. Hours later, she didn't suddenly say her ears were hurting. In fact, when we got in the car, she wanted to listen to her new Kidz Bop and sing pop songs, never once bringing up what just happened. Last night before bed, I got a Q-tip and showed her how to clean her new dolphins. That was our only real discussion about the whole thing.

It all kind of made me wonder if she really wanted it done. I guess I expected more hoopla, or a sign, or something. Something showing this was as big of a deal for her as it was for me.

This morning I was up early, downstairs with Hutch. I thought Parker was still asleep. We turned when we saw her gliding down the steps, dressed for the day. She'd already brushed her hair and teeth. Up and at 'em, doing everything by herself. That in itself was new. She was holding a Q-tip in one hand and the earring cleaner in the other.

She walked over and handed them to me.

"Miss Lynn said we have to do this every morning and night," she said. "I don't want you to forget."

The whole thing fell into place. Right then. It all clicked.

Parker hadn't been silent out of nervousness, she had been silent because she was absorbing the moment. She had waited and waited and dreamed about and thought over and waited and waited the past eleven months. When it finally came time, it wasn't that she was scared to have it done, she was just damned determined.

Maybe better yet, she was cool.

CR80

Please Parker, please continue having patience with me. Please, I beg of both you and your brother, keep teaching me as we go.

COMMENTS:

Dawn R. Just did this with my soon to be 6 year old and like Parker she has begged for them and also like Parker she did not say a word. I believe we are raising strong women.

Lori H. Kids are the great educators of us grown-ups, aren't they?

Marcia W. You need to put all these stories in a short book…I will buy the first copy!

To be continued . . .

AFTERWORD

Life is beautiful. Sometimes life also throws unexpected curveballs. Right as I was about to buckle down to work on this book, to change it from a bunch of thinly strung Facebook posts into more of a narrative, my Mom got really sick.

The breast cancer she had been living with for what seemed like forever advanced. She had been taking daily chemo pills with side effects that didn't cause visible changes, so even those of us around her most, who loved her best, almost forgot her constant battle. She never let it become a focal point.

But something had changed. She was feeling run-down. For weeks we wondered about her exhaustion; we didn't know it was her cancer storming a new organ. When we found out, the damage was already done. My mom and I were in the office listening together as her honest oncologist relayed tough news. He told us her breast cancer was in the process of shutting down her liver, and suggested she had six months left of life.

When we walked out, minds reeling, we did what many do in crisis-like moments: eat.

As we sat having lunch, trying to take in the information while picking at salads and burgers, we didn't know her cancer was sneaky and fast. We didn't know she wouldn't be alive four weeks later. We had no idea that would be our last meal together in a restaurant. Instead, we were focusing on the words "six months." We were having an upbeat discussion on what she wanted to accomplish in that time.

She eventually reversed my questions, asking what did I want in my next six months?

I told her about this book. I had tons of ideas, I said, like printing Facebook comments to make it a project many people were a part of (neither of us had seen that done before) and wanting to expand various posts to include a deeper peek into the news industry. I told her I wanted entries to be different lengths, but all to be easy-to-digest nuggets, quick words to read while sitting outside a ballet class or watching a child potty train. I told her it might be a book you could read at night to end your day with a laugh, or get someone for a baby shower to give some semblance of a real-life road map.

That conversation started an avalanche of stories between us.

I asked if she remembered when we lost Brown Bear. She didn't. I asked if she remembered how Hutch had no closet and I had dressed him in skinny jeans. Nope. I asked if she remembered our nightmare travel trip where Goldfish went all over the plane. She said she remembered me telling her about it, but had never read it online. It was then I realized that even if someone had read one post, or four, or three dozen, there were probably others they hadn't. My own mother hadn't kept track.

(The one she did remember? Putting a three-year-old, an eight-week-old, and a dog in a car and driving 1800 miles in one week. She compared it to her driving my brother Jay and me from Pinehurst, North Carolina, to Pennsylvania in a station wagon alone in the early eighties.)

I happily told my mom I wanted to name this book *Small Victories*, because that's how it all started. She liked that idea because, she said, the tiny successes in parenting were in complete contrast to my job which always seemed to be about big ones.

After that afternoon, Mom declined fast. Our family never left her side. During those long days and nights in a Hospice House, I'd have my laptop open, editing posts, reviewing comments, adding

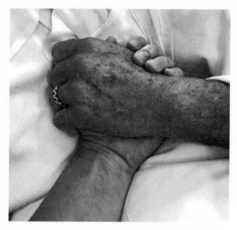

more here, taking stuff out there. I was writing this book about being a mom as I watched mine die. It felt very full circle.

We all know there comes a day where our parents lean on us more than we lean on them, but the transition metas-

tasized in front of my face. I was suddenly the mother to her and to my own kids, all at the same time.

Those days beside her bed also left ample time to think. I gratefully recalled that last lunch. Her words kept coming back in waves. She said she had always thought I'd author a book, but true to what

I wrote in this introduction, she couldn't believe I was writing nonfiction about raising children.

"You're going to do what I wish I would have done," I remember she'd said. It was an unintended compliment. "Maybe I'll just have to spend these next six months telling you all those childhood stories in my head so you have them in yours."

Sadly, Mom didn't get that chance. But through that one conversation she did give me the gift of endorsement and motivational push to create what you're holding.

A few days after her death, Wes and I took our family to the beach. One night the kids were asleep and I was up, sleepless, rereading old posts. Out of nowhere, I found a comment from my mom on *A Daughter*, where I'd written a love letter to Parker. Seeing her name on the screen took my breath away.

Her short message was perfect—it's included in this book (go to page 136). But seeing her words to me two years later, especially with the backdrop of the weeks we'd had before, made me want to publish this passion project not just for me, but for her. The book's dedication wrote itself right there.

I have continued to write monthly posts on my Facebook page: *www.facebook.com/WBTVMollyGrantham*. There's also more on: *www.MollyGrantham.com*.

I know my mom is enjoying these words about her grandchildren from high above, or wherever it is that spirits read.

—Molly

ACKNOWLEDGMENTS

There are lots of people to thank. The first are those who read these posts. I love Parker and Hutch, but I'm supposed to. I'm their mom. The fact many of you do, too, and comment in such personal ways by sharing your own lives is what makes this project special.

Next, to Wes. I love you. Thank you for always being you and for always letting me be me. Watching us cultivate Parker and Hutch into miniature versions of us is a beautiful thing. And to P & H—I hope you can someday appreciate the good, the bad, and the always real that's now documented. You've expanded the world in ways your father and I are still figuring out. I can say with unequivocal certainty, you are the most brilliant gifts the world has bestowed on us both.

To Betsy Thorpe, a Charlotte-based literary consultant who originally knew very little about television news, anchoring, or me, but who knows writing and how to navigate the world of publishing. Her patience and thoroughness was obvious at our first coffee-shop meeting. Thank you, Betsy, for leading the way.

To my brothers, Jay, Warner, and Stewart. Even though you three supposedly hate when I call you out publicly, I'll never apologize for shouting your importance. I wouldn't know what to do if the four of us didn't have each other.

To Gigi Jean, who despises technology and Facebook, but every time I'd print something out and have her read it old-school fashion, she'd take the time to give her sincere thoughts.

To Katrina, the best friend a girl could ask for, and the greatest mother I know.

To Melissa (the next biggest author you'll want to read), Kelly, and Kristen, for the freedom we gave each other to say whatever was needed. To Brian B., Sarah-Blake, Maddie, Kimmery M., Krista V. and Krista W. for constant encouragement. And to Morgan for every thought and read-through. Our friendship is unlikely perfection.

To Maya Myers for her copy editing and Diana Wade for her time, effort, and graphic artistry. (The cover!)

Also to the talented, talented, patient, and talented Mary Beth with Emby Taylor Photography. Our photo shoot with Parker and Hutch was one to remember. Thanks for being a professional image-grabber, but also a sympathetic mom. (See outtakes on *www. mollygrantham.com.*)

To my bosses—Scott, Dennis, and Kim—for supporting this project. You didn't laugh when I told you. That means more than you know. And an even bigger mention to all the workhorses inside our newsroom. You guys, our jobs are crazy. We leave our families and lives to walk into a building every single day and accomplish the impossible on unheard-of deadlines. Rarely do we fail. It's an insane, necessary industry, and we keep the call letters W-B-T-V standing for something strong.

Finally, to Keith. A man who uses words the way they are intended: to make you feel, and think. Thanks for the subtitle, and just because.

It's a crazy thing to see your name on the front of a book. It wouldn't have happened without everyone listed here.

Pinch me,
Molly

ABOUT THE AUTHOR

Molly Grantham is an Emmy-award winning anchor and investigative reporter in Charlotte, North Carolina. Besides her public and often nutty job, she also balances motherhood, social media madness, and the swirling cycle of life. She graduated from University of North Carolina at Chapel Hill and lives in Charlotte with her husband, two children, and Wonderdog Fisher. She doesn't suffer fools, is in love with the written word, and dreams of being a mermaid able to spend every day at the beach.